THE TASTE OF THE MIDDLE EAST

REVEALS THE UNDISCOVERED FOODS AND FLAVOURS OF AN ANCIENT CUISINE

A collection of 80 classic, authentic and well-loved recipes from a region rich in culinary traditions, shown in more than 360 stunning photographs

JENNI FLEETWOOD

southwater

This edition is published by Southwater, an imprint of Anness Publishing Ltd,
Hermes House, 88–89 Blackfriars Road, London SE1 8HA;
tel. 020 7401 2077; fax 020 7633 9499

www.southwaterbooks.com; www.annesspublishing.com

If you like the images in this book and would like to investigate using them for
publishing, promotions or advertising, please visit our website www.practicalpictures.com
for more information.

UK agent: The Manning Partnership Ltd
tel. 01225 478444; fax 01225 478440; sales@manning-partnership.co.uk
UK distributor: Grantham Book Services Ltd
tel. 01476 541080; fax 01476 541061; orders@gbs.tbs-ltd.co.uk
North American agent/distributor: National Book Network
tel. 301 459 3366; fax 301 429 5746; www.nbnbooks.com
Australian agent/distributor: Pan Macmillan Australia
tel. 1300 135 113; fax 1300 135 103; customer.service@macmillan.com.au
New Zealand agent/distributor: David Bateman Ltd; tel. (09) 415 7664; fax (09) 415 8892

ETHICAL TRADING POLICY
At Anness Publishing we believe that business should be conducted in an ethical and
ecologically sustainable way, with respect for the environment and a proper regard to the
replacement of the natural resources we employ.
As a publisher, we use a lot of wood pulp to make high-quality paper for printing, and that
wood commonly comes from spruce trees. We are therefore currently growing more than
500,000 trees in two Scottish forest plantations near Aberdeen – Berrymoss (130
hectares/320 acres) and West Touxhill (125 hectares/305 acres). The forests we manage
contain twice the number of trees employed each year in paper-making for our books.
Because of this ongoing ecological investment programme, you, as our customer, can have
the pleasure and reassurance of knowing that a tree is being cultivated on your behalf to
naturally replace the materials used to make the book you are holding.
Our forestry programme is run in accordance with the UK Woodland Assurance Scheme
(UKWAS) and will be certified by the internationally recognized Forest Stewardship Council
(FSC). The FSC is a non-government organization dedicated to promoting responsible
management of the world's forests. Certification ensures forests are managed in an
environmentally sustainable and socially responsible way. For further information about this
scheme, go to www.annesspublishing.com/trees

PUBLISHER: Joanna Lorenz
EDITORIAL DIRECTOR: Helen Sudell
EDITORS: Joanne Rippin and Elizabeth Woodland
PHOTOGRAPHS: Craig Robertson, William Adams-Lingwood, Patrick McLeavey,
Martin Brigdale
RECIPES: Ghillie Basan, Rosamund Grant, Rebekah Hassan, Soheila Kimberley
DESIGNER: Adelle Morris
COVER DESIGNER: Adelle Morris
EDITORIAL READER: Jay Thundercliffe
PRODUCTION CONTROLLER: Don Campaniello

© Anness Publishing Ltd 2007

Previously published as part of a larger volume, *Food and Cooking of Africa
and the Middle East*

The Publishers would like to thank the following picture libraries for the use of their images:
Corbis: pp 8, 9, 10 all, 11, 12b, 13, 14t. Travel Ink: pp 12t, 20t, 15bl.

NOTES
Bracketed terms are intended for American readers.
For all recipes, quantities are given in both metric and imperial measures and, where
appropriate, in standard cups and spoons. Follow one set of measures, but not a mixture,
because they are not interchangeable.
Standard spoon and cup measures are level.
1 tsp = 5ml, 1 tbsp = 15ml, 1 cup = 250ml/8fl oz.
Australian standard tablespoons are 20ml. Australian readers should use 3 tsp in place
of 1 tbsp for measuring small quantities.
American pints are 16fl oz/2 cups. American readers should use 20fl oz/2.5 cups in place
of 1 pint when measuring liquids.
Electric oven temperatures in this book are for conventional ovens. When using a fan oven,
the temperature will probably need to be reduced by about 10–20°C/20–40°F. Since ovens
vary, you should check with your manufacturer's instruction book for guidance.
The nutritional analysis given for each recipe is calculated per portion (i.e. serving or item),
unless otherwise stated. If the recipe gives a range, such as Serves 4–6, then the nutritional
analysis will be for the smaller portion size, i.e. 6 servings. Measurements for sodium do not
include salt added to taste.
Medium (US large) eggs are used unless otherwise stated.

Main front cover image shows Hot Spicy Prawns with Coriander – for recipe, see page 50

CONTENTS

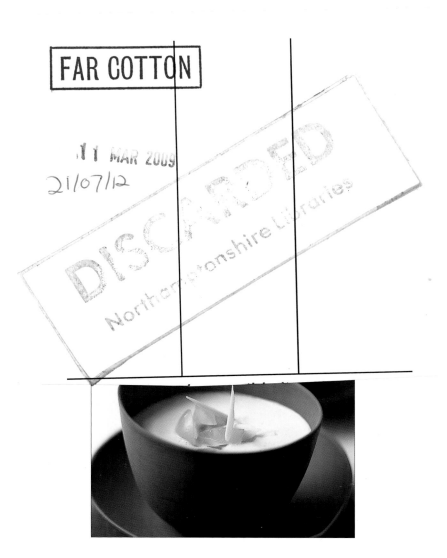

NF
09/07

INTRODUCTION

Eating today is an adventure in taste and discovery as we explore other cuisines and cultures through the food we enjoy. The Middle East is a vast area that has introduced a wide range of exciting flavours for us to discover. Many of their recipes are familiar to us, but there are still many more that are less well known. In this book we take a journey through this varied cuisine.

In the Middle East, sharing food and showing hospitality is a way of life, and many of the exciting foods enjoyed around the world today originated there, such as the well-known Tabbouleh, Kebabs and Falafel. Religion has played a part in shaping the culinary tradition: animals are slaughtered according to religious laws, and pork is eaten by neither Muslims nor Jews. Festivals, too, dictate what will be eaten and when. Lamb is a popular meat, cooked with vegetables and spices, and fish will be enjoyed in a variety of delicious ways. Sweet foods, too, are an adventure in themselves with deliciously sweet cakes and pastries filled with

Right: Hummus, a popular Middle Eastern dish can be used as a dip or a spread for sandwiches.

dried fruit and nuts, as well as fresh fruit desserts.

Rice, which was once a luxury ingredient grown along the northern borders of Persia around the Caspian Sea, is now one of the staples of Middle Eastern cuisine. Originally the diet consisted mainly of millet porridge, coarse bread, olives, figs, beans, cheese and milk.

Important ingredients nowadays include milk, honey, yogurt, cheese, fruit and vegetables, especially garlic and onions. Olive oil has long been recognized throughout the Middle East for its healthy properties. Meat and poultry are valued for their protein content, and if meat is not used, dried beans and other pulses are substituted.

Desserts are not common in the Middle East. The main courses tend to be very filling so fruit is generally the preferred choice at the end of the

meal. Sweetmeats are served on festive occasions, or when entertaining guests for tea.

Bringing together the authentic cooking styles and classic foodstuffs of this vast and diverse region, this book creates a colourful and enticing resource of recipes which share origins, ingredients and influences. An extensive introduction details the cooking traditions and ingredients. The following six chapters provide a wonderful selection of soups and appetizers, fish, lamb and beef, chicken and poultry, vegetarian dishes and accompaniments and refreshing fruit desserts and delectable pastries. There are so many traditional recipes to experiment with that the art of cooking becomes an integral part of the enjoyment of food.

Join us in a culinary tour of this exciting land, as you discover some of the varied and enticing dishes that make up the food and cooking of the Middle East.

Left: Many of the dishes that originated in the Middle East have become popular throughout the world thanks to an abundance of fruits and vegetables, flavourings and herbs and spices.

Opposite: Rice is served at many meals, either plain or with extra ingredients. Traditionally rice is a side dish – such as Shirin Polo, a colourful, sweet rice – but adding meat or chicken to it can make for a tasty main course.

HISTORICAL BACKGROUND

Exactly what constitutes the Middle East varies, depending upon which authority you consult. Some include the Maghreb – Algeria, Morocco and Tunisia – on the basis that these predominantly Muslim African countries share so much common ground with their eastern neighbours; some exclude Israel but include Afghanistan and some cling doggedly to the older term Near East, which used to comprise the Balkan States and the area of the Ottoman Empire. In this book we include Egypt's Middle Eastern culinary tradition. Therefore, the Middle East, the "belly of the Orient", includes Egypt, Iran, Iraq, Israel and the Palestinian Territories, Jordan, Lebanon, Saudi Arabia, Syria, Turkey, Yemen and the Gulf States of Kuwait, Bahrain, Qatar, the United Arab Emirates and Oman.

All these countries, with the exception of Israel, are strongly Islamic. In Iran, for example, 99 per cent of its population are Muslim; in Jordan the figure is around 96 per cent and in Kuwait around 85 per cent. Lebanon has a 60:40 Muslim:Christian split.

Iranians speak Persian (Farsi), Israelis Hebrew and Turks Turkish, but elsewhere the first language is Arabic. English is also widely spoken.

A FERTILE BEGINNING

Two mighty civilizations set the stage for the Middle Eastern story. Both developed in lush valleys and both owed their early stimulus to agriculture. The first of these was in ancient Egypt, in the extraordinarily fertile Nile Valley. The river flooded every year with predictable regularity. This laid down rich deposits of silt, which enabled wheat and other crops to be grown with ease. Beyond the river, irrigation made farming possible even in the surrounding desert, and the co-operation this required was one of the aspects that led to an ordered society.

In what is now Iraq, there was another mighty river valley. This was Mesopotamia, the land between the Tigris and Euphrates rivers. It formed part of a larger area known as the Fertile Crescent, which stretched in an arc from Israel to the Persian Gulf.

Here, as in Egypt, irrigation made large-scale agriculture possible. Nomadic hunter-gatherers became farmers, cultivating wheat, barley, figs, dates and pomegranates in the rich alluvial soil. There were marsh fowl and fish in the Delta, and these were incorporated into a diet that was not so very different from modern Iraqi fare.

FOOD FIT FOR PHARAOHS

The daily diet for most inhabitants of ancient Egypt was bread, vegetables and fruit, with perhaps a little fresh or dried fish. *Meloukhia*, a green vegetable that resembles spinach, was used for soup. The wealthier inhabitants might also have meat – duck, goose or maybe gazelle. Dried beans and lentils were widely eaten, just as they are today, and sweetmeats were popular. The earliest recorded Egyptian recipe is for a sweetmeat, a mixture of dates, walnuts and cinnamon, rolled into balls and coated with honey and ground nuts.

Below: Bedouin shepherds in Syria tend to their sheep.

A PATTERN OF CONQUEST

Egypt fell to Rome in 34 BC. Food played a role even in this event, for the conquest was prompted in part by Rome's desire for Egypt's vast grain reserves. In Mesopotamia, the Sumerians had long since been vanquished by the Akkadians, and a succession of new rulers took their place. Eventually, Mesopotamia, too, became a province of Rome. This pattern of events continued throughout the Middle East – with different principal characters – for centuries. Countries were invaded, bitter battles were fought and then there followed a period of relative calm and stability. The invading armies brought with them their favourite dishes and learned to like the local food as well, and when they swept on, as they inevitably did, they took with them the ingredients and cooking methods they had acquired.

This helps to explain why, wherever you go in the Middle East, you will encounter the same recipes. The names will be different and there will be subtle local nuances, but each will be recognizable. Of course, there are individual specialities, too. Iran (formerly Persia), for example, has a rich repertoire of rice dishes and a reputation for subtle spicing. The country was at one time on the famous Silk Route, so Persians had access to exotic ingredients to augment a diet that was already rich and varied.

Recipes of Arab origin, like Tabbouleh, and stuffed lamb with baba ganoush, were disseminated during the Arab Conquest, which began in the 7th century AD, when an army of the Prophet Mohammed's followers conquered all the lands that comprise present-day Syria, Lebanon, Israel, Iraq, Iran, Jordan and Egypt.

THE OTTOMAN EMPIRE

The cuisine of the Middle East may have been shaped by these disparate influences, but it was the Turkish Ottomans who refined it. They came to power at the beginning of the 14th century. Within 150 years they had conquered Constantinople (now

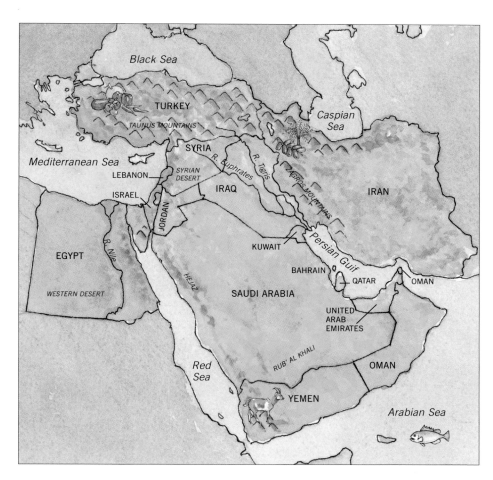

Istanbul), the former Byzantine capital, and built the fabulous Topkapi Palace. Banquets at the palace became legendary. Food was prepared by a team of cooks, including butchers, bakers, pastry cooks, confectioners, yogurt and cheese makers and experts in pickling and preserving vegetables and fruit. Only the finest ingredients were used. The empire that eventually stretched from Cairo to Budapest, and from Tripoli to Baghdad, provided plenty of ingredients and inspiration.

FOREIGN INFLUENCES

After the First World War, which signalled the end of the Ottoman Empire, Britain administered Palestine, Transjordan, Iraq and Egypt, whereas France took control of Lebanon and Syria. France had the greater impact, not so much in the way of introducing typical French dishes, but rather in refining the cooking and presentation of local specialities.

Omani cuisine reveals several foreign influences. Between the 17th and 19th centuries, Oman was a powerful seafaring nation that rivalled Portugal and England in the Gulf, the Indian Ocean and the coasts of India and East Africa. Returning sailors introduced spices from Zanzibar and curries from India. The food in Yemen has an Indian flavour, too, thanks to interaction with Indian merchants. Chillies are used more widely in Yemen than anywhere else in the Middle East.

Israel has a dynamic and very varied cuisine. Since the establishment of the State of Israel in 1948, hundreds of thousands of Jews from many countries have emigrated there, each national group bringing their traditional dishes to add to the Kosher tradition. Chopped liver from Alsace, polenta fritters from Italy, cherry soup from Hungary, *pierogi* from Poland – all these plus a host of typically Middle Eastern dishes are to be found on the menu.

A CUISINE STEEPED IN TRADITION

Social mores and religious observance play a large role in the way food is prepared, cooked and served in the Middle East. Muslims and Jews both abstain from eating pork, and there are strict laws governing the way permitted animals are slaughtered. Custom dictates how food is served and to whom, and there are largely unspoken but firmly entrenched traditions surrounding the role of the host and the offering of hospitality.

MUSLIM RELIGIOUS OBSERVANCE

Islamic doctrine is enshrined in the Koran, or Qur'an. The word literally means "recitation" and is held to be the word of God (Allah) as dictated to the Prophet Mohammed by the Angel Jibril (Gabriel). There are five articles of faith, the first of which is the doctrine that there is only one true God and his name is Allah. The prime observances or duties Muslims must perform include public acknowledgement of Allah and of Mohammed as his prophet; praying five times a day; giving alms; making a pilgrimage to Mecca at least once in a lifetime and fasting from sunrise to sunset every day during Ramadan.

Below: A stall in the famous night-time marketplace Jema al Fnr, Marrakesh, Morocco, renowned for fabulous food.

Food that may be eaten is described as halal (lawful). This includes beef, goat, lamb and poultry slaughtered in the permitted manner. Pork is taboo. Game may be eaten in certain circumstances, provided the hunter is a Muslim or the child of a Muslim. Fish with scales are halal, provided they were alive when taken from the water. This also applies to prawns (shrimp), but lobster, crab, shellfish and fish that lack scales, such as shark, are not allowed. All alcohol and other stimulants are forbidden.

Above: Bedouin women eat after they have served the men, sitting outside their tent in the Sinai Desert.

In addition to the Koran, Muslims honour the Hadith, or Tradition, a record of the sayings of Mohammed, together with accounts by others of how the Prophet himself lived. The Hadith offers additional guidance on how adherents should conduct themselves, and has quite a bit to say on the subject of food. Some of the tenets are simply good practice; for example, Muslims are

The Laws of Kashrut

Observant Jews also adhere to strict dietary laws. Only certain meats and types of fish are permitted, and animals must be dispatched by a *shochet,* or ritual slaughterer. Blood must be removed from the animal immediately after slaughter. Dairy foods and meat must not be cooked together, and if meat has been eaten, a period of time must elapse before any type of dairy food can be consumed. Wine, beer and spirits are permitted, with some limitations. There are special observances for the Sabbath, and for festivals such as Pesach (Passover) and Purim.

advised to wash fruit thoroughly but not to peel it before eating, water should be sipped, not gulped, and no Muslim should drink from a cup with a cracked rim. Food must not be wasted. Any leftovers must be fed to animals or used in another dish. This has led to the development of some intriguing recipes, including Fattoush, a salad composed largely of stale bread and vegetables.

THE HONOURED GUEST

The offering of hospitality is deeply ingrained in the Arab psyche. As an old proverb declares: "Three things are no disgrace to man, to serve his guest, to serve his horse and to serve in his own house." In Bedouin society, this concern for the well-being of a guest is particularly marked. A traveller seeking food and accommodation will not be turned away. Even an enemy must be taken in for 48 hours if need be, and then given safe conduct as he proceeds on his journey.

In Bedouin society, as is the Arab pattern, men and women eat separately. The women prepare the food, but do not eat until after the men have finished their meal. A Western female guest will be accorded the same courtesies as her husband, however. The meal begins with the ceremonial washing of hands. Guests sit cross-legged on the carpeted floor of the tent and the meal is placed in the centre. Traditionally, this is likely to be *mansaf*, Jordan's national dish. The word means "big tray", which is an accurate description. A very large tray is covered with several sheets of flat bread. On top of this is piled rice mixed with roasted pine nuts and almonds, and over that is heaped pieces of succulent cooked lamb. The whole dish is bathed in a yogurt sauce, which is regularly replenished as the meal proceeds. No utensils are used. Instead, everyone eats with the right hand, the left being reserved for personal hygiene.

Before taking the first bite, prayers may be said. During the meal, the guest will be encouraged to eat his fill, and more than his fill. When everyone has eaten, coffee will be served and it is

accepted form for a guest to drink several small cups before signifying – with a wave of the empty cup – that he has had enough.

If there are obligations on the host, there are also expectations of the guest. He may be offered a special delicacy, like the eyes or testicles. This titbit must not be refused. It is expected that a guest will eat heartily and show appreciation. Finally, a guest should not overstay his welcome. As Mohammed said: "It is not right for a guest to stay so long as to incommode his host."

MODERN TRENDS

Although the Bedouin model of hospitality may not be encountered very often by the average visitor to the Middle East, kindness and courtesy

Above: Ancient farming methods in rural areas of the Middle East reflect the enduring social traditions of the culture.

remain a mark of even the most ordinary encounter. Meals will be prepared with elaborate care, because to take time and trouble honours the guest. Cooking will probably begin early in the day, so that there will be plenty of tasters – the mezzes – for the visitor to sample before moving on to the main course. The meal will be ample and the host will be satisfied only if waistbands are put under strain. Guests will be offered the best chairs and everything will be done to make them feel at home. In contemporary households, men and women may eat together, and serve alcohol, even in Muslim homes.

DAILY EATING PATTERNS

In the Middle East, it is invariably the women who cook, clean and care for children. This is the case even when the woman works full time, as more and more women do. In Israel, the pattern is altering somewhat, particularly among young couples where both are wage earners, but in Arab-Muslim societies in particular, women are the ones who go to market, prepare the food and, in many cases, serve their menfolk first before they and their children have their meal. Convenience foods, like finely ground or minced meat for meatballs and kebabs, ready-to-use shredded pastry and filo pastry, prepared mezzes and salads from shiny supermarkets, make women's lives easier, but many still prefer the old ways, and buy their produce from the *souk* or market.

THE DAILY DIET

In most of the Middle East, the pattern of meals is more or less the same. The day begins early for many people,

because it makes sense to get as much work done as possible before it becomes unbearably hot.

For the business person, breakfast might simply consist of a bowl of yogurt with some honey or preserves, or a couple of bite-size pastries bought from the bakery on the way to the office. Many people start the day with bread, olives, soft cheese, tomato and cucumber, but the traditional breakfast, enjoyed from Alexandria to Aqaba, is *foul*. The word can be spelled in many different ways, but the dish is always basically the same: cooked dried broad (fava) beans mashed with oil and lemon juice. The Jordanians add some chopped chilli and the Lebanese like to stir in chopped fresh coriander (cilantro). In Turkey, a favourite breakfast dish is *menemen*, which

Below: The markets of the Middle East are full of fresh fruit and vegetables, which are bought on a daily basis.

Above: Dinner in a Jordanian restaurant, where food is served from a large plate set in the centre of the table.

consists of a thick tomato sauce spiked with chilli. Hollows are made in the sauce and an egg is broken into each. When the eggs are cooked, the dish is topped with crumbled feta cheese and served with flat bread.

Lunch is eaten between 1.00 and 3.00 p.m. Rural dwellers often make this their main meal, but in the cities, people prefer a snack and will often choose two or three mezzes with some bread and perhaps a piece of fruit. Those eating at home might plump for a bowl of beef and herb soup with yogurt, or spinach and lemon soup with meatballs. There'll always be bread, even if all it accompanies is a little cheese and a few olives.

Hummus, which is chickpea purée, is popular, as is the broad bean equivalent, byesar. Office workers may choose some street food, such as Falafel served in pitta bread with onion slices and tomatoes.

The evening meal can be eaten at any time between 8.00 and 11.00 p.m. This is generally the main meal of the day for city people. It will begin in a leisurely fashion, with the serving of mezzes. The main course might be anything from grilled (broiled) fish or poultry to a meat dish. Offal (variety meats) is very popular in the Middle East, or a simple stew may be offered. If you are in Iran, this is likely to be a Khoresh, served over rice. Bread will accompany the meal and there will probably be several salads, all served with a dollop of yogurt on the side. Dessert will be fresh fruit – perhaps a slice of chilled melon, or just a single perfect peach. If it is a special occasion, a sticky pastry such as baklava or kodafa may be served, or a piece of basbousa, the coconut halva beloved of the Egyptians. Creamy rice puddings, scented with rosewater or spiced with cardamom are also popular.

Above: Street food has an important role in the Middle East, and stalls laden with vast arrays of sweetmeats are common.

RAMADAN

During the month of Ramadan, the ninth month in the Islamic calendar, Muslims fast. Most families rise very early, long before daybreak, to share a meal – *sahur*. When it is light enough (when "the white thread can be distinguished from the black thread of dawn") the fast begins and all who are able must refrain from eating or drinking until the sun goes down.

In the evening the fast is broken with another meal – *iftar*. This is very much a family time, although guests are very welcome, and the meal is often shared with others, especially those considered to be less fortunate than their hosts. Ramadan ends with the festival of Eid ul-Fitr, when gifts are exchanged and parties held.

MIDDLE EASTERN INGREDIENTS

The food of the Middle East, like that of the Mediterranean, is fundamentally healthy. There are regions where meat is the mainstay, and the diet is high in animal fats, but most people eat plenty of vegetables and fruit, fresh fish and a relatively small amount of meat, which is generally grilled (broiled) over an open fire. For energy, they rely on slow-release carbohydrates like pulses. The extra-sweet pastries for which the region is famous are eaten as treats with coffee or tea, rather than as daily desserts, so don't have the devastating impact on the diet that might be assumed.

The exciting world of Middle Eastern ingredients is encapsulated in the open-air markets throughout the regions, where the senses are stimulated by the sight of glossy purple aubergines (eggplants), bright red cherries, yellow quinces, baskets of fresh greens and sacks of lentils. The aroma of lemons, warm spices and fresh coffee fills the air. Having filled your basket, you are invited to munch on a handful of nuts or sample a few marinated olives before stepping into a shop for more mysterious items, like pomegranate molasses, *pekmez* and *zahtar*.

Below: Turkish coffee, thick, black and sweet, is served after dinner, or with a sweetmeat in the afternoon.

FAVOURITE FOODS

Wheat is the favourite grain, and bread is always on the table. There is a wide variety of breads, including leavened and unleavened loaves and flat breads. All the bread must be eaten; leftovers will be incorporated into a tasty dish. Rice, introduced from India, is also widely eaten, especially in Iran. As well as forming a main part of the meal, it is also used to make stuffings for vegetables and vine leaves and there are numerous recipes for rice mixed with vegetables or lentils. Short-grain rice is used for puddings and soups.

The most popular meat is lamb, followed closely by chicken, which is cooked in a variety of ways, perhaps spatchcocked and cooked over a brazier – to be enjoyed as a street food – or simmered in yogurt until tender. Middle Eastern cooks also specialize in the cooking of offal (variety meats). Everything from liver and kidneys to trotters and testicles is eaten, and some of the tastiest spiced dishes are made from these apparently unpromising ingredients. Fish is very popular in coastal regions, especially in Turkey and

Above: Fresh vegetables locally grown are an important part of cooking in the Middle East. Here an Egyptian farming family pick their peppers.

Below: These distinctive oval-shaped olives have been grown in the Middle East for centuries.

Oman, and freshwater or sea fish are generally preferred to shellfish. Many recipes for cooking fish include spicy sauces or herb stuffings, and nuts and fruit may also be added to complement the flavours of the fish.

Vegetables and fruits are important in their own right, but are also used in stews and ragoûts. Particularly popular are aubergines, courgettes (zucchini), spinach and green beans. There is a wide range of salads, often served with labna (white cheese) or yogurt. Salads always appear as part of mezze – a selection of small dishes served as a first course or to accompany a main dish. Garlic is popular in Mediterranean lands, but elsewhere in the Middle East it is regarded as being rather brash and is often omitted from recipes.

Luscious Middle Eastern fruits, such as melon and pomegranate, are enjoyed after a meal, and many fruits, both fresh and dried, will also be cooked with savoury foods. Deliciously sweet Middle Eastern pastries, however, are traditionally served with afternoon coffee and not as a dessert. Coffee and tea are widely drunk. Both are served without

Below: Dried fruits are used widely in the Middle East, as snacks and desserts, and as an ingredient in both sweet and savoury dishes.

Above: Dried beans and peas are staple ingredients and are used widely in many traditional dishes.

milk. Fruit drinks and drinks that are based on yogurt are on offer everywhere, but alcohol is less widely available due to the Muslim prohibition on its consumption.

The following pages introduce and explain some of the regions' raw ingredients, used for everyday cooking throughout the Middle East, as well as traditional breads, pastries and drinks.

Nations of nut lovers

Almonds, cashew nuts, pine nuts, peanuts, hazelnuts and pistachio nuts are extremely popular in the Middle East. Nuts serve as snacks, street food and as the basis for sauces like *tarator* – a lemon, garlic and pine nut mixture traditionally served with fish. Ground nuts are used, often with dried fruits, in stuffings for poultry and as fillings for sweet pastries. *Ma'amoul*, for example, can have a walnut and cinnamon filling, a pistachio and rosewater filling, a ground almond and orange flower water filling or any combination of these, with dates or other dried fruit. Nuts are often combined with seeds, as in the Egyptian snack food *dukkah*, which is a mixture of crushed roasted hazelnuts or chickpeas with sesame and coriander seeds.

Many of the ingredients featured are widely available in general stores and supermarkets; for some of the others you might need to find a specialist supplier, or make a substitute.

Below: Ras al hanout is a spice mix used throughout the Middle East.

WHEAT, RICE AND BEANS

First cultivated in Mesopotamia some ten thousand years ago, wheat is an extremely important crop in the Middle East, where some kind of bread is eaten at every meal. Rice is also widely eaten, while beans add variety and protein.

WHEAT

An unfussy cereal, wheat will flourish in a range of climates, although it does best in cooler conditions. In most areas of the Middle East wheat is therefore a winter crop. The main areas of cultivation are Turkey, central Iran, coastal Lebanon and Israel, northern Syria and Iraq, Jordan and the Nile Delta.

There are two main varieties: bread wheat and durum wheat, which is used for pasta and semolina. What distinguishes bread wheat is its high gluten content. This elastic protein substance is what makes leavened bread maintain its rise. It does this by strengthening the dough so that it traps the carbon dioxide produced when yeast ferments.

Bulgur wheat

Sometimes described as the world's first processed food, bulgur wheat is durum wheat that has been ground into particles after being cleaned, lightly boiled, dried and hulled. Before use, it needs only brief cooking, or can simply be soaked in boiling water. In the Middle East it is widely used in pilaffs, salads – especially Tabbouleh – and the

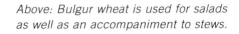

Above: Bulgur wheat is used for salads as well as an accompaniment to stews.

legendary Lebanese dish, Kibbeh. Bulgur wheat is also the basis of several sweet dishes, and is mixed with fermented yogurt and then dried to make another pelleted product, *kishk*, which is used to thicken stews.

Whole-wheat grains, called *kamh* in Egypt, are boiled in milk and water to make a porridge-like mixture, which is generally eaten with yogurt and honey.

Semolina and wheat

Also known as *smeed*, semolina is coarsely milled durum wheat. The Berbers use it to make a thick gruel, and it is also an ingredient in some desserts and cakes, especially halva. Couscous is made from semolina.

Wheat flour is used for breadmaking, and is also the basis of the thin, crisp pastry that we know as filo or phyllo. The Turkish version, yufka, comes in

Below: Fine yufka, made from semolina and used for pastries.

various thicknesses. Fine yufka is used for pastries, while the thicker type of dough is used for a stuffed bread called *gözleme*.

RICE

Long-grain rice arrived in the Middle East from northern India and Afghanistan, which helps to explain why fine varieties like basmati are generally preferred in countries like Iran and Iraq. In Egypt, where rice was traded through Alexandria's "Pepper Gate" towards the end of the first century AD, the grain was originally perceived as a medicinal

Below: Couscous is perhaps the most common ingredient in the Middle East.

Below: Long-grain rice, such as this Iranian rice, is the most popular variety.

Below: Semolina is used to make porridge, puddings and desserts.

food and used to treat stomach ailments. Today, Egyptians eat around 43kg/94lb per person annually, making them among the world's highest consumers. Despite this impressive figure, the richly fertile Nile Delta produces so much rice (three times the average yield) that Egypt is the only Middle Eastern country with a surplus. Most of this goes to its close neighbours: the Middle East is the world's third biggest importer of rice, after Europe and Brazil.

Middle Eastern cooks use rice in a wide variety of ways, but no nation is as adept at cooking it as the Iranians. Rice is grown along the Caspian coast. There are several varieties, including the much-prized *domsiah*. In Persian cooking (still called Persian, despite the name of the country being changed to Iran), light, fluffy rice with each grain separate is a speciality. Rice is so important that the stew served with it, Khoresh, is somewhat dismissively referred to as a sauce. Persians have also perfected the art of cooking rice so that a crisp crust forms on the base of the pan. This is the tahdeeg, which is broken up and served to guests.

BEANS AND LENTILS

Beans, peas and lentils have been cultivated and dried in the Middle East for centuries, and today's pulses (legumes) were developed from wild plants that originally grew in the lands bordering the Eastern Mediterranean. There are numerous mentions of pulses in the Bible, the most famous of which describes the incident when Esau sold his birthright for "a pottage of lentiles". A direct descendant from that famous bowl of lentil soup is *mujaddarah*, a lentil and rice stew that is traditionally eaten by Christian communities in Lebanon during Lent. The name means "smallpox" and it refers to the way in which the lentils stud the white rice and create a spotted appearance.

Dried beans and peas

Of the many varieties of dried bean eaten in the Middle East, broad (fava) beans are probably the most common.

Above: Hummus, made from chickpeas, is a popular mezze dish.

A small brown variety called ful or foul is the basis of Egypt's national dish, ful medames. The soaked beans are cooked very simply, with onion skin and whole eggs, and the thick broth that results is eaten throughout the Middle East for breakfast, lunch, dinner and as a street snack.

In Israel, white haricot (navy) beans are widely used, especially in the long-simmered stew known as Cholent. Black-eyed beans (peas) are popular, too. Chickpeas are extensively used throughout the region, particularly for

Below: Dried haricot beans from Israel, where they are a particular favourite.

Hummus and Falafel. Small and khaki-coloured, chickpeas look a little like pale hazelnuts. They retain their shape when cooked and are delicious in a spinach salad. Chickpea flour is frequently used as a thickener.

Lentils

Cheap, nutritious and easy to cook, lentils are widely used in the Middle East. The small red split lentil is favoured in Egypt and Syria, whereas Lebanese cooks tend to prefer the green or brown varieties.

Green shoots for Christmas
As Christmas approaches in the Lebanon, Christian children layer chickpeas, lentils and beans between pieces of cotton wool. These are placed on saucers and watered regularly until the shoots are about 15cm/6in long. When the family sets up the nativity scene, the shoots are placed in the manger and on the floor of the stable to represent hay.

HERBS AND SPICES

Judicious use of herbs and spices is the secret of many Middle Eastern dishes. Although there are some countries where fiery food is enjoyed, such as Yemen, the preference tends to be for mild, warm spices and cool, fresh herbs such as mint and parsley.

The Middle East is also home to some fascinating spice blends. Until recently these were little known outside their countries of origin, but the universal demand for new taste sensations has led to their being packaged and marketed worldwide.

Mint

Mint is an essential fresh herb in Middle Eastern cooking. It is used with lamb dishes, as an ingredient in salads and vegetable dishes, as a flavouring for yogurt sauces and with fruit. A sprig of fresh mint is often added to a glass of the sweet black tea that is such a feature of Middle Eastern life.

Parsley

You are unlikely to find curly parsley in the Middle East, but the flatleaf variety is extremely popular. This is particularly true in Lebanon, where cooks add extravagant handfuls of chopped parsley to dishes like Tabbouleh. In Iran, flat leaf parsley is one of the herbs used in *kuku sabzi*, a baked egg dish, rather like a large omelette, which is served to celebrate the New Year.

Coriander

This herb, also known as cilantro, is a member of the parsley family native to the Middle East and Mediterranean. In Middle Eastern cooking it is the leaves

Below: Flatleaf parsley is used generously in dishes such as tabbouleh.

Above: Mint is used in enormous quantities in Turkey, for tea and salads.

and seeds that are most commonly used. Fresh coriander has a spicy citrus and ginger flavour, quite different from that of flat leaf parsley, which it resembles. The small, round seeds look like pale, creamy peppercorns; they are used whole in pickles, but are more often roasted and ground. Freshly ground coriander has a mild, warm flavour that is discernible in many Middle Eastern dishes, especially meatballs and stews.

Dill

Although most people associate dill with Scandinavia, the herb is actually native to western Asia and is hugely popular in the Middle East. The feathery, fern-like leaves and seeds have a flavour

Below: Thyme is a woody herb that retains much of its flavour when dried.

redolent of caraway. Dill goes particularly well with fish, but in the Middle East is also popularly used with vegetables. Fresh dill is often strewn into rice dishes, and is frequently partnered with broad (fava) beans.

Thyme

The aroma of wild thyme is familiar to anyone who has journeyed to the Eastern Mediterranean. In the Middle East, the herb is known by its Arabic name of *zahtar*. Confusingly, the same name is also used to describe a popular spice mix based on thyme.

Cardamom

Ancient Egyptians chewed cardamom pods to whiten their teeth and sweeten their breath. The spice grows mainly in India, and reached the Middle East via Iran. It consists of small fleshy pods, which reveal tiny seeds when split. Green, white (bleached) and black cardamoms are grown, the former being the most popular. The seeds have a warm, slightly citrus flavour. Coffee flavoured with cardamom – *gahwa* – is a favourite drink among Arabs, and is served with considerable ceremony.

Cumin

A native of Upper Egypt and the Mediterranean, cumin has been a favourite spice in the Middle East for centuries. The ancient Egyptians were reputedly very fond of it, and cumin seeds have been found in the tombs of the pharaohs. Today, cumin is widely cultivated throughout the Middle East. Turkey and Iran are particularly important producers of cumin seeds,

Below: Dill is used in fish and vegetable dishes and goes well with broad beans.

Above: Ground cinnamon

Above: White cumin

Above: Black cumin seeds

Above: Ground sumac

with Iran being a source of black cumin as well as the more familiar brownish-yellow variety.

Paprika

Made from a mild red sweet pepper, this sweet, pungent spice is more popular in Turkey than other parts of the Middle East.

Saffron

Used sparingly, this costly spice imparts a delicate flavour and yellow colour to foods, but it can taste musty if overdone. The familiar thin red threads are the stigmas of a crocus that grows well in Iran and Turkey. The threads are usually steeped in a liquid before being used. Ground saffron is also available.

Cinnamon

The rolled bark of an evergreen tree related to the laurel, cinnamon is a sweet, warm spice. It was known to the ancient Egyptians, who used it in religious ritual as well as in the kitchen.

Below: Harissa, a Tunisian spice mix, is also used in the Middle East.

Modern Middle Eastern cooks enjoy its mellow fragrance in both sweet and savoury dishes. In Turkey it is used to flavour tea, while in Azerbaijan it is an important ingredient in beef soup. Cinnamon is also mixed with ground nuts to make a variety of sweet pastries.

Other spices

Sumac is derived from the red berries of a bush that grows throughout the Middle East. The dried berries can be used whole, but are more often ground or cracked, then soaked in water. The liquid that results has a slightly sour, fruity flavour, which gives a pleasing astringency to stews. The berries can be ground and used as a rub for chicken, steaks or kebabs, and is also sprinkled over salads.

Hawaij

This earthy spice blend comes from Yemen. It tastes great in stews, soups and sauces and is also good sprinkled on vegetables before they are roasted. Try it as a rub for lamb chops that are to be grilled (broiled) or barbecued. You can buy ready mixed hawaij in packets, but it is easy to make:

Place 30ml/2 tbsp black peppercorns in a mortar and add 15ml/1 tbsp caraway seeds, 5ml/1 tsp cardamom seeds and several pinches of saffron threads. Use a pestle to grind the mixture.

Add 10ml/2 tsp each of ground cumin and turmeric. Mix together. Use as indicated in recipes. Surplus hawaij should be kept in a sealed jar in a cool, dark place.

Tamarind is another souring agent. It is not as widely used in the Middle East as it is in India, but a drink made from it is popular. Mahlebi is a ground spice, made from the kernel found inside the stone of a small black cherry that grows in Turkey and elsewhere in the Middle East. It has a nutty flavour, suggestive of almonds and cherries, and is used in cakes, breads and pastries.

Spice mixes

The Middle East is a source of some excellent spice mixes, many of which are now available in the West. Harissa, actually a North African mix, is used in couscous, and is widely available. Try baharat, a warm blend of paprika, nutmeg and cardamom that tastes good in meat and vegetable dishes. Kabsa, from Saudi Arabia, is a fiery mixture that typically contains cayenne pepper, cinnamon, cumin, black peppercorns, nutmeg, cardamom, lime rind, cloves and coriander. Zahtar is a blend of sesame seeds, thyme and sumac.

Below: Zahtar is a dry spice mix often used to flavour an olive oil dip.

OLIVES AND OLIVE OILS

There's something miraculous about a tree that can live for hundreds of years on poor soil, baked by the sun and denied regular rainfall, yet still produce fruits that are not only delicious in their own right, but also yield an exquisite oil. Perhaps this explains why olives have always had such cultural and spiritual significance. The olive branch is an ancient symbol of peace and the oil is used to anoint adherents of several religions. Olive oil was used in ancient Egypt as part of the embalming process and is central to the ritual of Christian baptism. Jars of cured olives have been found in the tombs of the Pharaohs, presumably placed there to give them sustenance in the afterlife. Mohammed advised his followers to eat the olive's oil and massage it over their bodies.

The olive tree has been cultivated for more than six thousand years. Whether it originated in Syria or Crete is a matter of constant conjecture (and heated argument) but there is ample evidence of its being traded in both these places by 2500 BC. The Minoans introduced olives and olive oil to mainland Greece. Soon, thanks to Phoenician traders, the fruit and oil were both widely known throughout the Mediterranean region.

Freshly picked olives are extremely bitter and have a metallic taste. When it was discovered that preserving them made them infinitely more palatable, their popularity was assured. The oil,

meanwhile, had myriad uses: in lamps, it burned beautifully without smoking; when perfumed, it made a fine medium for massage; it had proven medicinal qualities and could even be used to lubricate chariot axles (and was reputed to have made it easier to manoeuvre the huge stones into position when the pyramids were built). And, of course, it could be used as a marinade, as a cooking medium and as a preservative.

The Roman empire played an important role in disseminating the olive, introducing it to countries it had conquered, and expanding olive cultivation in lands where it was already well known, such as Palestine. It was

Above: Market stalls all over the Middle East sell a wide variety of olives.

the Romans who developed the screw press, used for the efficient extraction of olive oil. Meanwhile, in more remote Arab lands, farmers continued to tend their trees as they had done for generations, harvesting the olives in due season, preserving them or pressing them to remove the oil.

Olive oil was not the only cooking medium in ancient times. Arabs also favoured oils derived from nuts of various types and used sesame, sunflower and corn oil. In many areas, especially among nomadic tribes,

Below: Black olives have been left on the tree to ripen the longest.

Below: These distinctive brown olives are very popular in the Middle East.

Below: Fresh olives have to be preserved before they are edible.

animal fats such as sheep tail fat and butter were preferred, since these could be extracted or churned from the milk of their herd animals.

Today, however, olive oil is the main type of oil used for cooking and as a condiment in much of the Middle East, especially in Syria, Turkey, Jordan and Lebanon. Syria and Turkey are both important oil producers – not in the same league as Spain, Italy and Greece, but still in the top ten of producers.

TYPES OF OLIVE

There's always a crowd around the olive stall in a Middle Eastern market. Everyone has a favourite fruit, and there will often be intense discussion as to the virtues of this glossy black olive or that smaller green one, or whether olives in brine taste better than those that have been cured in salt. The colours of the olives are an indication not of the variety, but rather of ripeness. Immature olives are green, and at this stage the flavour is quite acrid. The fruit must be treated with lye before being preserved. As the olives ripen, the colour changes to khaki, brown, red, purple and finally black. The longer the olives stay on the tree, the sweeter they become. Black olives also yield more oil than green ones.

Table olives – as distinct from olives grown specifically for their oil – are generally preserved in brine, although

Above: Virgin olive oil is prized for its distinctive flavour.

some will be packed in oil, cured in salt or merely packed in water. Graded by size, the smallest weigh around 3.2g/$\frac{1}{16}$ oz whereas the largest, aptly described as "supercolossal", tip the scales at around 15g/$\frac{1}{4}$oz.

OLIVE OIL

Increasingly, olive oils are being appreciated for their individual flavours. Some are mild and buttery; others are fruity or have a distinctly peppery flavour. Colours range from palest yellow to deep, intense green. Some oils come from a single type of fruit, others are blends. Middle Eastern oils are now attracting the attention of discriminating

> **Marinated olives**
>
> For a tasty snack or mezze, try marinated olives. Tip 450g/1lb black olives into a bowl. Pour over 30ml/2 tbsp red wine vinegar, then add 1 garlic clove, cut into slivers, with 2 whole red chillies and 3–4 slices of lemon. Mix well, then spoon the olives into a large jar or several smaller jars, and pour in enough olive oil to cover them. Cover tightly and leave for 2–3 weeks at room temperature.

Above: Various types of oil, from very dark green virgin olive oil at the front, flanked by sesame oil to the left, and a lighter olive oil to the right.

buyers. Highly regarded extra virgin oils are Mishelanu from Galilee in Israel and Rashaya from Lebanon. Sadoun is an interesting oil from Jordan.

Grades of oil

Olive oil is graded in terms of its acidity level and how many pressings it has had. In addition to the categories below, there are blended oils and oils flavoured with aromatics and herbs.
• Extra virgin olive oil, which comes from the first pressing of the olives, has low acidity and a superior flavour. It is not recommended for frying, but is the perfect choice for salad dressings.
• Virgin olive oil has a slightly higher level of acidity than extra virgin and is also a first-pressed oil.
• Pure olive oil has been refined and blended and has a lighter, more subtle flavour than virgin olive oil. It is suitable for all types of cooking and can also be used as a dressing.

FISH, MEAT AND POULTRY

The diet of the average man or woman in the Middle East, unless he or she lives in a modern city, is likely to be limited to what is fished, raised or grown in the immediate vicinity. Fish is a valuable addition to the diet and is often more affordable than meat, which is saved for special occasions. Lamb is widely enjoyed in many different forms. Chicken is also popular; it is common to buy live birds from market, which are dispatched and prepared at home.

FISH

Most of the countries in the Middle East have extensive coastlines. In many parts a fisherman can still make a decent living and those who fish the eastern Mediterranean have better hauls than their counterparts to the west. The Arabian Sea also yields a rich harvest, whereas the Red Sea is the source of colourful reef fish, as well as king prawns (jumbo shrimp) and tasty flat lobsters. Oman has some of the finest fishing territories in the Middle East, and shark, tuna and grouper, are landed in its waters. From the Black

Below: Grey mullet, a favourite Middle Eastern fish, are often cooked with dill.

Sea come delicious fresh anchovies, while the Caspian is home to the sturgeon, from which comes the expensive delicacy, caviar.

Shellfish are not as widely eaten as sea fish or freshwater fish. This is largely because Jews who observe the dietary laws of Kashrut must abstain from eating any kind of shellfish and crustaceans, as well as squid, octopus and certain types of fish. Muslims may not eat lobster or crab, although prawns are permissible if taken from the water alive. The Koran also forbids the eating of fish that do not have scales, such as shark or catfish. The following are some of the more popular varieties of fish available and eaten in the Middle East.

Red mullet

Common in Mediterranean waters, red mullet are considered to be among the best tasting sea fish. Perhaps that's one reason why they are given the grand title of Sultan Ibrahim in the Middle East. Red mullet are often cooked whole, either in the pan or – more often – on the barbecue where they may be wrapped in vine leaves to protect the flesh. Egyptians like to serve red mullet with a sauce made from chopped hazelnuts and pine nuts.

Grey mullet

A favourite way of cooking this fish is to stuff it with dill – a herb that is extremely popular in the Middle East – and grill (broil) it, dousing it with arak or raki (both spirits) from time to time.

Red snapper

Around the Arabian Sea, these handsome fish are often called job or jobfish. Red snapper are generally pan fried or baked. The flesh is robust enough to compete with quite strong flavours, and Egyptians like to bake red snapper in a lightly spiced tomato sauce.

Tilapia

The succulent white flesh of tilapia is quite sweet, and goes well with fruity flavours. In Egypt and Israel the fish is sometimes marketed as St Peter's fish, which can be confusing, as John Dory has the same nickname.

Trout

This is a popular fish, especially in Turkey and Iran, where the rivers and lakes of the Alborz mountains north of Tehran are well stocked with trout, and fishing is a popular pastime.

Below: Brown trout and rainbow trout are both farmed extensively throughout the Middle East.

Caviar and bottarga

The finest caviar is said to be beluga, from the large Caspian sturgeon; oseotre comes from the Danube sturgeon (also found in the Caspian) while sevruga comes from the small Caspian sturgeon. Sadly, all these fish are now endangered species, with beluga on the critical list. Many people now prefer to buy bottarga (shown below), the salted and dried roe of the grey mullet.

MEAT

The quality of meat available varies considerably, but Middle Eastern cooks have devised numerous ways of making even the least promising cuts taste good. All parts of the animal are eaten, and some offal (variety meats) is considered to be a delicacy.

Lamb is the meat of choice throughout the Middle East. Very little pork is consumed, since neither observant Jews nor Muslims may eat it, and beef's availability is limited, largely because there is not enough suitable grazing for the best beef animals, nor is the climate ideal. Goat (kid) is eaten, as is – on occasion – young camel. Game is also served, particularly in Iran, which has wild deer, and some of the biggest wild boar in the world.

Beef

There has been a gradual shift towards more beef consumption, particularly in larger, more cosmopolitan cities, and in Iran and Iraq, where beef and lamb are often used interchangeably. This is particularly true in the case of Koftas (meatballs). Beef is also eaten in stews, such as the Persian Khoresh.

Lamb

Used in a variety of recipes, lamb is roasted, chargrilled, baked, braised, stewed and used as a filling. Ground or minced lamb is baked as a loaf or transformed into meatballs, which are

Above: Lamb is used in a great variety of dishes throughout the region.

cooked in a rich tomato sauce or threaded on to skewers and cooked on an open fire. Very finely ground or pounded lamb, mixed with bulgur wheat, is the basis for the famous Lebanese and Syrian dish Kibbeh. Lamb kidneys are enjoyed skewered or sautéed, and lambs liver, often cooked with paprika and garlic, is a favourite dish in Turkey.

POULTRY

Spatchcocked chickens are a favourite street food basted with oil and lemon juice, with herbs or a sprinkling of sumac. Roast chicken is popular, too, and is often stuffed with spiced dried fruit and nuts. Chicken is cooked in yogurt for the Persian dish Tah Chin, which makes it beautifully tender. Perhaps the Middle East's most famous chicken dish is Khoresh Fesenjan, from Iran – a colourful mixture of chicken,

Below: Jointed chicken is used in many different Middle Eastern dishes.

Roast pigeon, Egyptian-style

Pigeon is always popular in Egypt. This dish, Hamam Mashwi, is one of the simplest ways of cooking young birds, the marinade makes the flesh and keeps it moist.

4 plump young pigeons
1 large onion, finely chopped
juice and zest of 2 lemons
30ml/2 tbsp olive oil
salt

Preheat the oven to 180°C/ 350°F/Gas 4. Clean the pigeons, and rinse them under cold water. Drain and pat dry with kitchen paper. Place side by side in a shallow dish and strew with the chopped onion. Grate the zest of the lemons over the birds, then use your hands to work the onion and lemon rind into the skin. Mix the juice from the lemons with the olive oil and pour over the pigeons. Cover and leave to marinate in a cool place for 4–6 hours.

Place the pigeons, with the marinade, in the roasting pan, sprinkle with salt and roast for 45–55 minutes, or until the birds are fully cooked, basting frequently.

pomegranates and walnuts. Also popular, especially in Egypt, is pigeon. In the Nile Delta pigeons are plump and of a good size. Egyptians like them roasted or grilled (broiled).

Below: Shin of beef is an ideal cut for slow stewing in a casserole.

Below: Pigeon is farmed in the Nile Delta and is enjoyed roasted or grillled.

FRESH FRUIT AND VEGETABLES

Middle Eastern markets are a kaleidoscope of colour. Baskets of tomatoes, piles of dusky purple aubergines (eggplants), scented lemons, fat peaches, exotic pomegranates and okra pods are all there for the buying. Shopping for ingredients, especially fruit and vegetables, is a serious business for the Middle Eastern cook. First a circuit must be made of the market to locate the finest produce, and then the niceties must be observed – an inquiry as to the health of the stallholder's sister, perhaps, or a remark about the weather. After this, honour is satisfied and the purchase is completed.

FRUIT

It is traditional throughout the Middle East for a meal to conclude with fresh fruit. A slice of chilled melon, perhaps, a bowl of cherries or just a perfect peach. In winter, such fresh fruit as is available may be added to a dried fruit compote, or a rice pudding topped with berries picked earlier in the year and preserved for just such an occasion. Fresh fruit is used in salads, as when pomegranate arils are mixed with fresh greens, or added to stews. Lemon is the linchpin of Middle Eastern cooking, but other types of citrus are important, too. From Israel, one of the world's most important citrus producers, come Jaffa oranges, white and pink grapefruit and kumquats. Lebanon is famous for soft fruits, Iran for cherries and melons and

Above: Apricots are a particular favourite in the Middle East.

Turkey for superb figs. Baalbek, the former Phoenician city close to Beirut, is known for its magnificent apricots. It is said that their flesh is so fine that when the fruit is held up to the light, the stone can be seen inside. Apples are grown in the more temperate areas; bananas, pineapples and mangoes grow in coastal regions with good irrigation.

Figs

Turkey is one of the world's leading exporters of this delicious fruit. Smyrna figs are sweet and succulent, with golden flesh, while Mission figs are deep purple, with red flesh. Figs are delicious on their own, but can also be split and opened out to hold a nut filling, baked with honey or served with white cheese.

Below: Quinces have a delectable fragrance and mild, sweet flesh.

Quinces

These are fabulous fruit that originated in Turkestan and Persia. In colder climes, they do not achieve their full potential, but when they are placed in the heat they fill the air with their exquisite perfume.

Quinces make delicious jams and jellies, but are also good in meat dishes, and stuffed quince – *dolmeh beh* – is excellent. This Persian dish involves coring the fruit, packing it with a meat and split pea mixture and cooking it in a sweet-and-sour sauce.

Pomegranates

On the tree, pomegranates look like polished cricket balls, but cut them and you find jewelled treasure. Inside the fruit, each seed is encased in a translucent sac of pulp. These arils, as they are called, are deliciously refreshing, but getting at them is no mean feat. It is important to avoid the bitter pith, so the arils must either be picked out individually, using a pin, or pressed into a bowl and then picked over by hand. Middle Eastern cooks use pomegranate seeds in salads, in savoury dishes and in desserts. They are inordinately fond of pomegranate juice, which they sweeten and serve very cold. Juicing a pomegranate is easy – just press it down very gently on a citrus squeezer.

Below: The jewel-like seeds of the pomegranate are sharp and refreshing.

Below: Figs are eaten fresh, or cooked in a variety of delicious desserts.

Above: This flavoursome, ridged tomato is grown in the Lebanon.

VEGETABLES

There's something almost decadent about the vegetables of the Middle East. No prissy broccoli or prudish peas here, but instead voluptuous violet aubergines (eggplants), perky peppers, courgettes (zucchini) – so prolific as to be positively indecent – and shiny round tomatoes, exquisitely sweet, thanks to being grown in bright sunshine in unpolluted desert air. Also on the menu are artichokes, fresh broad (fava) beans, long thin cucumbers, leafy spinach and glossy pumpkin, which is served as a vegetable and also transformed into a candied sweet. Okra, with its mucilaginous texture, isn't to everyone's taste, but the pods are delicious in a chickpea stir-fry or a tomato stew. Peppers are widely used, and are just one of the vegetables that Middle Eastern cooks like to stuff with rice and herbs or a savoury meat mixture. And let's not forget salads: these are universally popular and, thanks to modern farming methods, even the driest desert regions are now capable of producing crisp, fresh greens. A salad will often be delivered to the restaurant table along with the menu, so that diners can take the edge off their appetites while they make their meal choices. Salads form part of

Desert truffles

Oil is not the only treasure to lie beneath desert sands. From Egypt to Iraq, a rich harvest of truffles is gathered each year. Called *terfas* by the Bedouin of the Western Desert, and *kamaa* in Syria, they are not so strongly flavoured as European truffles, but are still delicious – and much more affordable.

every mezze spread, often with yogurt dressings, and are also served as separate courses in their own right. Most of the vegetables that feature in Middle Eastern cooking will be familiar to cooks everywhere, but the following warrant a little more explanation.

Artichokes

As soon as globe artichokes are in season they are seized upon by cooks eager to use them for mezze or in main-course dishes. When very young, before the choke has formed, the entire artichoke is edible.

Okra

Also called ladies' fingers, or *baamieh* in Arabic, okra pods are shaped like slim, tapering lanterns. If the pods are cooked whole, as in a stir-fry, they stay crisp, with no trace of slime, but cut them and cook them in a stew, and the

Below: Aubergines come in several shapes and sizes, and can also be white or purple and white in colour.

Above: Artichokes are used extensively in Middle Eastern mezzes and salads.

rows of seeds release a sticky liquid. This has the effect of thickening the sauce, but in a glutinous way that is not to everyone's taste. Okra goes well with tomatoes, chillies and ginger.

Aubergines

Known as eggplants in America and *brinjals* in India, these tasty vegetables come in several different shapes and sizes. They are especially appreciated in Turkey, a nation that is said to have more than two hundred recipes for preparing them.

Middle Eastern recipes often recommend salting aubergines to draw out some of their bitter juices, but this is seldom necessary in the West, where the vegetables available are usually young and tender.

DRIED FRUIT AND FLAVOURINGS

Most Arabs have a sweet tooth, which is hardly surprising when you consider that sweet, succulent dates have been part of their diet since childhood. Dried fruits and nuts are favourite snacks, and the penchant for mixing sweet with savoury flavours means that dried fruits are a feature of both meat dishes and desserts. Fruit syrups are highly concentrated and can be overwhelming. For more subtlety, select one of those signature Middle Eastern flavours: rosewater or orange flower water.

POPULAR VARIETIES OF DRIED FRUIT

Middle Eastern cooks often use dried fruit to add a touch of sweetness to a savoury dish. A mixture of nuts and dried cherries, apricots and barberries might be used to stuff a chicken, for example, or meatballs might be studded with the tiny black currants referred to as bird grapes. In

Above: Once dried and packed, dates will last for months.

Azerbaijan, dried fruit is the basis of a beef soup flavoured with mint and cinnamon, whereas in Israel dried apricots and prunes are cooked with vegetables to make *tzimmes*. Raisins, sultanas (golden raisins) and currants

Above: Sun-dried apricots.

are produced in the Mediterranean region, especially in Turkey.

Dates

Plump and succulent, dates are among the most delicious of fruit, whether you enjoy them fresh from the tree or dried. The date palm is extensively cultivated throughout the Middle East. Iraq leads the world in date production, closely followed by Iran and Saudi Arabia. For centuries, dates have been an important food for Arab tribesmen and traders. An excellent energy source, they are easily portable and provide valuable minerals, making them a good match for the fermented milk and occasional meat meals that are standard desert fare.

There are more than three hundred date varieties, classified by how much moisture they contain.

Soft dates are deliciously sweet and juicy. Arabs like to eat them before they are fully ripe, when the flesh is still crunchy and the flavour has a tart undertone. Ripe dates of this type taste like toffee and are almost as sticky. Popular varieties include the Khadrawi, which comes from Iraq, and the Bahri, from Israel and Egypt. Another date that is widely grown in Egypt is the Halawi, which is soft fleshed and slightly chewy. The

queen among soft dates is, however, the Medjool, a Moroccan variety that is now cultivated in the Middle East, California and South Africa. Plump and voluptuous, this deep red-coloured date has little fibre and a superb flavour.

Semi-dry dates are firmer than soft varieties and have a lower moisture content. Deglet Noor, Dayri and Zahidi fall into this category. These dates are often sold in boxes, with what look like plastic twigs for winkling them out.

Dry dates are hard and fibrous, almost nutty in texture. These are the dates traditionally eaten

Clockwise from top left: sultanas, currants, and raisins.

by nomadic Arabs, who refer to them as bread dates. The dryness is natural, but they are sometimes dried even more so that they can be ground to a powder.

Below: Two different sizes of dried figs.

Compressed dates are dried fruit that have been tightly packed together in blocks. Very high in sugar, they are largely intended for baking, and are often softened in water before use.

Dried figs

Turkey is the world's major producer of dried figs. Smyrna figs from Izmir are particularly prized, but the purple Mission figs are popular too. Travellers to Turkey will often see the flattened fruit, suspended in loops from reeds or spread on hurdles to dry in the sun. Drying concentrates the natural sugars, which in turn helps to preserve the fruit. Tiny dried figs are eaten like sweets in the Middle East; larger fruits are stuffed and baked, or stewed in water scented with rosewater to make a compote.

Dried apricots

Called *zard-alu* or "yellow plum" by the Persians and *mishmish* in Arabic, apricots have been sun-dried for centuries in the Middle East. In addition to being dried individually, apricots are compressed to make qamar el-deen, thin sheets of fruit leather that make a drink when dissolved in boiling water. During Ramadan, serving this drink often signals the end of the daily fast.

Dried barberries and sour cherries

An Iranian speciality, dried barberries are often sprinkled over pilaffs or added to stews. The berries themselves are a small, wild, red fruit, about the size of redcurrants. They are too bitter to eat fresh but become sweeter dried. Dried sour cherries are used to flavour stews in Turkey, Iran and Syria.

Below: Dried sour cherries.

Above: Flower waters: on the left orange flower water, on the right rosewater.

Dried pomegranate seeds

When dried, the arils, or seeds, of pomegranates can be used in place of raisins in desserts and also to flavour vegetables and lentil dishes in Iran and Iraq. The pomegranates from which the arils are extracted are a sour variety, not suitable for eating raw.

FRUIT SYRUPS

Popular throughout the Middle East, fruit syrups are used in marinades, meat dishes and desserts, but their primary function is as a flavouring for long, cold drinks. A small amount of syrup, topped up with iced water or soda (carbonated) water makes a sweet but refreshing beverage.

Also known as *visne*, cherry syrup is the sweetened juice of sour cherries. It is sold by street sellers and makes a pretty drink when diluted over ice.

Made from concentrated grape juice, *pekmez* is remarkably sweet, despite the fact that the only sugar comes from the grapes themselves. Used sparingly, pekmez can add an interesting flavour to chicken and also works well in a dried fruit compote. Also known as *halek*, *dibis* is a concentrated date syrup. Popular in Israel, it is widely sold

in jars, but can also be made at home by soaking dried dates in water until plump, then boiling them in water until soft. After being puréed, the date mixture is then cooked again until it reduces to a thick, syrupy paste to be diluted with water. Also called pomegranate molasses, this syrup is a delicious product with the consistency of treacle. It goes well in dressings and has long been an important ingredient in Persian cooking.

FLOWER WATERS

Rosewater has a unique flavour, delicate yet always clearly discernible. Distilled from the petals of the pink damask rose, it is used throughout the Middle East, in cakes, desserts and ice creams. Perhaps best known for its role in *lokum* (Turkish delight), rosewater is the perfect partner for iced melon.

Orange flower water is made from bitter orange blossoms. It is used to flavour pastries and cakes, and is the basis for the well-known Lebanese "café blanc", which is actually a beverage made by boiling the essence with water.

Below: Clockwise from bottom right: date syrup, sour grape juice, pomegranate paste, rosehip syrup and sour cherry juice.

BREADS, PASTRIES AND CAKES

The expression "daily bread" is nowhere more accurate than in the Middle East, where peasant workers eat over 1kg/2¼lb a day and it is enjoyed at every meal. Cakes and pastries, for which the region is equally famous, are as lavish as the loaves of bread are plain. Many of them are extremely sweet: the perfect accompaniment to a cup of strong, black Turkish coffee.

BREADS

Although bread is of enormous value merely as sustenance, it also plays a role in religious observance throughout the Middle East. The baking and buying of bread is a social event, too. Many Middle Eastern housewives work together to bake for themselves and the community, or take their risen dough to the village baker.

Above: A selection of the bread sold each day all over the Middle East.

Above: Pide.
Below: Simits.

Below: Ekmek.

Muslims are enjoined to treat bread with respect. It should be torn, not cut with a knife, which would show disrespect to what they regard as a gift from Allah. When it is brought to the table it should be eaten immediately, taking precedence over other foods. Any bread remaining at the end of a meal must be used, perhaps in the delicious salad known as Fattoush. Even crumbs must be gathered up and either eaten by those present or fed to animals. This rule – that no food must be wasted – is fundamental to the teachings of Islam.

The royal bakers who prepared food for the pharaohs are known to have made more than 30 different types of bread. Across the whole of the Middle East today, the number is much higher. Flat breads, such as *lavash*, plump loaves such as *hashas*, sheets, crusty bread rings, puffy individual breads that reveal pockets when split – the range of both leavened and unleavened loaves is vast. What they have in common is that they must be eaten fresh. Bread stales rapidly in the Middle East, but this is not a problem since bread is baked at home or in a bakery at least once a day.

Right: A pile of lavash, *the flat bread used to scoop up food at mealtimes.*

Pide

This is the Turkish version of the bread the Greeks call pitta. It can be shaped in rounds or be slipper-shaped. When baked in a very hot oven, the dough puffs up so that the centre remains hollow, making each individual bread the perfect receptacle for a salad, some cheese or a few chunks of grilled (broiled) lamb slid from a skewer. *Pide* is often served with mezzes.

Aiysh

This is similar to *pide*, but smaller and thicker. This Egyptian bread, which has been made in the same way for thousands of years, is found throughout the Middle East. It is generally made with wholemeal (whole-wheat) flour and ranges in shape from 15cm/6in rounds to ovals of up to 38cm/15in. In Yemen the bread is known as *saluf*; in Jordan and Palestine as *shrak*; and in Syria as *aiysh shami*.

Ekmek

The word simply means "bread" in Turkey, but usually refers to a large round or oval leavened bread made simply from a plain white or wholemeal dough. *Sutlu Ekmek*, for example, is made by arranging a circle of round rolls around a central roll in a baking pan so that they rise and stick together to form a single loaf.

Khoubz

Virtually identical to *aiysh*, this flat, slightly leavened bread is popular in the Levant and Arabian peninsula. Originally made with finely ground wholemeal flour similar to chapati flour, it is now more often made using white flour.

Simits

Shaped in golden bread rings, *simits* are traditionally coated with sesame seeds, and are sold in the streets. They look like bagels and are made in the same way, being first poached in water and then baked.

Barbari

These flattish white breads from Iran come in various sizes and shapes, and are dimpled or slashed to give the surface a fretwork effect. They may be brushed with oil before being baked, and spiced versions are often topped with cumin or caraway seeds.

Lavash

This pancake-thin bread originated in Armenia, but is now popular throughout the Middle East. It can be round, oval or square, and is made in various sizes, the largest sheets measuring up to

60cm/24in across. A large *lavash*, placed in the centre of the table, will serve the entire party. Guests tear off as much as they need and use the bread as a wrap or for scooping up sauce.

Challah

Traditionally made for the Jewish Sabbath or for religious festivals, this braided bread has a deep brown crust. The dough is made using eggs and vegetable oil, which gives the baked bread a texture somewhere between that of a brioche and a soft white loaf.

PASTRIES AND CAKES

Middle Eastern pastries are the stuff of dreams. Whisper-thin pastry, cooked to crisp perfection, is filled with some of the most delicious concoctions imaginable. Ground pistachio nuts and cardamom, dates and almonds, candied apricots, coconut and semolina custard – these are just some of the many possibilities. Further flavouring comes from lemon or lime rind, warm spices or the subtle yet pervasive taste of flower waters. Syrup or honey is often poured over the hot pastries as they emerge from the oven, soaking in to become sensationally sticky. Eat something like this at the end of a large meal and it seems over-sweet, over-indulgent and

Above: M'hanncha are one of the many varieties of sweet pastries available.

decidedly over the top. But cut a small portion and enjoy it in the middle of the afternoon with a cup of strong, black Turkish coffee, as people in the Middle East do, and its appeal becomes immediately obvious.

Pastries are popular street foods and it is not unusual to see a vendor performing a seemingly impossible balancing act as he hurries to his pitch with a large tray of pastries on his head. Among the most popular treats is *kodafa*, a rich cheesecake made with an unusual shredded pastry called *kadaif*. The *kodafa* is strewn with pistachio nuts and served with a honey and saffron syrup scented with orange flower water.

It is in Israel and other communities with large Jewish populations that the largest variety of cakes are to be found. Almond cakes, Russian poppy seed cake, Polish apple cake and honey cake are the legacy of those who left the lands of their birth to settle in Israel. Many of them are made without flour; groundnuts and matzo meal are used instead, with beaten egg whites as the raising agent. This allows them to be eaten during Pesach, when leavened foods are forbidden.

COFFEE, TEA AND SOCIAL DRINKING

Aside from water, coffee and tea are the most widely drunk beverages in the Middle East. Each has its own rituals regarding preparation and serving. Tea and coffee ease introductions, cement friendships and oil the wheels of commerce. Anyone contemplating making a major purchase is liable to be offered a cup of coffee or glass of tea to ease the pain of parting with money. Muslims may not drink alcohol, so fresh fruit drinks and beverages made from fruit syrups are freely available, as are several milk- or yogurt-based beverages.

COFFEE

There's some disagreement about whether the coffee plant originated in Ethiopia or the Middle East, but Yemen can certainly lay claim to being one of the first countries to cultivate coffee on a large scale. The southern part of the country is suited to coffee production, and the terraced slopes of the mountains are criss-crossed with coffee plants, each row protected from the harsh sun by a row of poplar trees. The arabica coffee from the south-western tip of the Arabian Peninsula is rich and mellow, with underlying acidity and a chocolate aftertaste. It was originally

Below: Turkish coffee will have a froth on the top if it has been made correctly.

exported through the port of Mocha. This not only gave it its name – Yemen Mocha – but also led to the word "mocha" being used to describe any chocolate-coffee flavour.

The coffee trade in Yemen reached its peak in the 17th and 18th centuries. Today it is in decline, due in part to increased demand for *qat*. This leafy narcotic, a source of a natural amphetamine, is regularly chewed by a large percentage of the population, and coffee bushes are constantly being grubbed up so that more *qat* (*Catha edulis*) trees can be planted.

None of this has diminished the popularity of coffee, however. Arabs, particularly those who live in Yemen and Saudi Arabia, brew the beverage without sugar, in kettles or pots called *dallahs*. The coffee is then poured into tall pots, many of which are exquisitely crafted, before being served in cups.

Turkish coffee

This thick, sweet beverage is not a specific type of coffee, but rather a method of preparation that was developed in the Middle East in the early 16th century. Traders introduced it to the Ottoman court, and the proper preparation of Turkish coffee soon became a vital skill. Women in the harem were instructed in the art, and

Above: Mint tea is a refreshing drink in the heat of the summer.

young girls had to become expert if they hoped to find suitable husbands.

A small open pot with a long handle is used for brewing Turkish coffee. Generally made of tin-lined brass, it is called an *ibrik* or *cezve*. Legend has it that the desert sands become so hot during the day that coffee can be brewed directly on them as evening falls, but the more usual method is for the pot to be placed on the stove or in the embers of a fire. Any arabica coffee can be used, but it must be ground very finely, so that it resembles a powder. Ground cardamom or ginger can be added, giving a distinctive flavour.

When making Turkish coffee, the aim is to allow the brew to bubble up several times without boiling over, so that a thick froth forms on top of the liquid. When the coffee is poured out, it should be left to stand briefly so that the ground coffee sinks. It forms a sludge on the bottom of the cup, which should not be drunk.

The amount of sugar in the coffee varies. Technically there are six levels of sweetness, but in practice most people ask for *sekerli* (very sweet), *orta sekerli* (with a little sugar) or *sekersiz* (without sugar). These are Turkish terms; elsewhere in the Middle East different classifications are used. Arabic or Bedouin coffee, on the other hand, is

Above: Fruit juices (clockwise from front) rosehip, pomegranate and peach.

Above: Sugar cane juice is a very sweet drink served in the Middle East.

Above: Ayran is made of yogurt that has been diluted with water.

drunk without sugar. This green or grey liquid, with its slightly bitter taste, is enjoyed in Syria and Jordan.

TEA

Although coffee is widely drunk, especially in Lebanon, tea, or *chai,* is the favourite drink in many parts of the Middle East. Like coffee, it is served with considerable ceremony, and – again like coffee – it is drunk without milk and with sugar. It is the custom in some areas for the recipient to place a cube of sugar between their front teeth, and sip the tea through it. Tea is often flavoured with mint or with spices such as ginger or cinnamon. In Turkey, herb and fruit teas made from sage, rose hips and apples are on sale.

SOFT DRINKS

Fresh fruit juices are widely available from stand-up juice bars, but long, cold drinks made from concentrated fruit syrups topped up with iced water are even more popular. In Egypt, hibiscus juice – often called "red tea" – is a favourite drink, along with apricot juice, tamarind juice and a drink made from dates. Cherry juice is popular in Iran, whereas orange and tamarind juice, either separately or as a mixture, are enjoyed in Israel. Liquorice juice is a more unusual choice, found in Egypt

and Jordan, and there are several extremely sweet drinks, including honey water and sugar cane juice, both of which are served ice cold.

YOGURT AND MILK DRINKS

Yogurt, diluted with water, is a favourite thirst-quencher for the desert Bedouin. In Syria and Turkey, this drink is called *ayran.* It is often served with mint. *Salep* is a hot milk drink flavoured with cinnamon and thickened with sahlab, ground orchid root. *Boza* is a fermented wheat drink that has a reputation for being especially nourishing and healthy.

Wines of the Middle East

The main wine-producing countries of the Middle East are Israel, Lebanon and Turkey. Historically, Israel has been best known for kosher wine, but now produces Cabernet, Sauvignon Blanc, Grenache and Semillon. Lebanon's wine industry is centred on the Bekkah Valley and produces some fine red wines, largely derived from Cabernet Sauvignon grapes. Turkey produces a considerable amount of wine, and quality reds from Thrace, Anatolia and the Aegean region are highly regarded.

ALCOHOLIC DRINKS

The Koran forbids the drinking of alcohol. In some countries this taboo is strictly enforced. In Saudi Arabia, for example, the sale and/or consumption of any type of alcohol is strictly prohibited, and strict penalties are imposed on anyone caught flouting the law. Elsewhere in the Middle East, the situation is somewhat more relaxed. In Jordan, for example, alcohol is available in many hotels and restaurants, but drinking alcohol in public can cause deep offence. Turkey is more liberal, and has Western-style bars and pubs, though these remain largely male preserves. Beer, brewed under licence, is available, as is wine.

The most popular spirit is raki, a potent aniseed-flavoured drink distilled from grain, which clouds when mixed with water, a phenomenon that has earned it the nickname *aslan sutu* (lion's milk).

Right: The favourite spirit in the Middle East is aniseed-flavoured raki.

SOUPS AND APPETIZERS

In the Middle East, the first course is seen as a main component of the meal, rather than simply a morsel to tempt the appetite, and in Iran, soup is held in such high regard that the kitchen is known as "the house of the soup maker". The art of the appetizer reaches its apogee in Lebanon, where a mezze consists of dozens of different dishes, balanced to offer a feast of colours and flavours.

CHILLED ALMOND AND GARLIC SOUP WITH ROASTED CHILLI AND GRAPES

THE COLD AND CHILLED SOUPS OF NORTH AFRICA ARE ANCIENT IN ORIGIN AND WERE ORIGINALLY INTRODUCED TO MOROCCO BY THE ARABS. THIS PARTICULAR MILKY WHITE SOUP HAS TRAVELLED FURTHER WITH THE MOORS INTO SPAIN. HEAVILY LACED WITH GARLIC, IT IS UNUSUAL BUT DELICIOUSLY REFRESHING IN HOT WEATHER, AND MAKES A DELIGHTFUL, TANGY FIRST COURSE FOR A SUMMER LUNCH PARTY.

SERVES FOUR

INGREDIENTS
130g/4½oz/¾ cup blanched almonds
3–4 slices day-old white bread,
  crusts removed
4 garlic cloves
60ml/4 tbsp olive oil
about 1 litre/1¾ pints/4 cups
  iced water
30ml/2 tbsp white wine vinegar
salt

To garnish
1 dried red chilli, roasted and
  thinly sliced
a small bunch of sweet green grapes,
  halved and seeded
a handful of slivered almonds

1 Place the blanched almonds in a blender or food processor and process to form a smooth paste. Add the bread, garlic, olive oil and half the water and process again until smooth.

2 With the motor running, continue to add the remaining water in a slow, steady stream until the mixture is smooth with the consistency of single (light) cream. Add the vinegar and salt.

3 Transfer the soup to a serving bowl and then chill for at least 1 hour.

4 When the soup is chilled, stir gently before serving into individual bowls. Garnish each bowl with the sliced roasted chilli, halved grapes and a few slivered almonds.

COOK'S TIP
Almonds can be bought ready-blanched, but you can also blanch them yourself in boiling water. To blanch almonds using a microwave oven, place them in a bowl, cover with boiling water and microwave on High for 2 minutes. Drain, and peel off the skins.

Energy 352Kcal/1459kJ; Protein 8.6g; Carbohydrate 13.8g, of which sugars 3.4g; Fat 29.5g, of which saturates 3.1g; Cholesterol 0mg; Calcium 102mg; Fibre 2.8g; Sodium 110mg.

CINNAMON-SCENTED CHICKPEA AND LENTIL SOUP WITH FENNEL AND HONEY BUNS

THIS THICK LENTIL AND VEGETABLE SOUP, FLAVOURED WITH GINGER AND CINNAMON, VARIES FROM VILLAGE TO VILLAGE AND TOWN TO TOWN. IT IS BELIEVED TO HAVE ORIGINATED FROM A SEMOLINA GRUEL THAT THE BERBERS PREPARED TO WARM THEMSELVES DURING THE COLD WINTERS IN THE ATLAS MOUNTAINS. OVER THE CENTURIES, IT HAS BEEN ADAPTED AND REFINED WITH SPICES AND TOMATOES FROM THE NEW WORLD.

SERVES EIGHT

INGREDIENTS

    30–45ml/2–3 tbsp smen or olive oil
    2 onions, halved and sliced
    2.5ml/½ tsp ground ginger
    2.5ml/½ tsp ground turmeric
    5ml/1 tsp ground cinnamon
    pinch of saffron threads
    2 x 400g/14oz cans chopped tomatoes
    5–10ml/1–2 tsp caster
      (superfine) sugar
    175g/6oz/¾ cup brown or green
      lentils, picked over and rinsed
    about 1.75 litres/3 pints/7½ cups
      meat or vegetable stock, or water
    200g/7oz/1 generous cup dried
      chickpeas, soaked overnight,
      drained and boiled until tender
    200g/7oz/1 generous cup dried broad
      (fava) beans, soaked overnight,
      drained and boiled until tender
    small bunch of fresh coriander
      (cilantro), chopped
    small bunch of flat leaf parsley, chopped
    salt and ground black pepper
For the buns
    2.5ml/½ tsp dried yeast
    300g/11oz/2¾ cups unbleached
      strong white bread flour
    a pinch of salt
    15–30ml/1–2 tbsp clear honey
    5ml/1 tsp fennel seeds
    250ml/8fl oz/1 cup milk
    1 egg yolk, stirred with a little milk

1 Make the fennel and honey buns. Dissolve the yeast in about 15ml/1 tbsp lukewarm water. Sift the flour and salt into a bowl. Make a well in the centre and add the dissolved yeast, honey and fennel seeds. Gradually pour in the milk, using your hands to work it into the flour along with the honey and yeast, until the mixture forms a dough – if the dough becomes too sticky to handle, add more flour.

2 Turn the dough out on to a floured surface and knead well for about 10 minutes, until it is smooth and elastic. Flour the surface under the dough and cover it with a damp cloth, then leave the dough to rise until it has doubled in size.

3 Preheat the oven to 230°C/450°F/ Gas 8. Grease two baking sheets. Divide the dough into 8 balls. On a floured surface, flatten the balls of dough with the palm of your hand, then place them on a baking sheet. Brush the tops of the buns with egg yolk, then bake for about 15 minutes, until they are risen slightly and sound hollow when tapped underneath. Transfer to a wire rack to cool.

4 To make the soup, heat the smen or olive oil in a stockpot or large pan. Add the onions and stir over a low heat for about 15 minutes, or until they are soft.

5 Add the ginger, turmeric, cinnamon and saffron, then the tomatoes and a little sugar. Stir in the lentils and pour in the stock or water. Bring the liquid to the boil, then reduce the heat, cover and simmer for about 25 minutes, or until the lentils are tender.

6 Stir in the cooked chickpeas and beans, bring back to the boil, then cover and simmer for a further 10–15 minutes. Stir in the fresh herbs and season the soup to taste. Serve piping hot, with the fennel and honey buns.

Energy 376Kcal/1594kJ; Protein 18.7g; Carbohydrate 66.4g, of which sugars 12g; Fat 5.9g, of which saturates 1g; Cholesterol 2mg; Calcium 181mg; Fibre 8.6g; Sodium 70mg.

IRANIAN BEEF AND HERB SOUP WITH YOGURT

THIS RECIPE IS CALLED AASHE MASTE IN IRAN. IT DATES FROM ANCIENT PERSIAN TIMES, WHEN SOUP WAS SO IMPORTANT THAT THE WORD FOR COOK WAS ASH-PAZ, LITERALLY "MAKER OF THE SOUP".

SERVES SIX

INGREDIENTS
2 large onions
30ml/2 tbsp oil
15ml/1 tbsp ground turmeric
90g/3½oz/½ cup yellow split peas
1.2 litres/2 pints/5 cups water
225g/8oz minced (ground) beef
200g/7oz/1 cup long-grain rice
45ml/3 tbsp each chopped fresh
  parsley, coriander (cilantro),
  and chives
15g/½oz/1 tbsp butter
1 large garlic clove, finely chopped
60ml/4 tbsp chopped fresh mint
2–3 saffron threads dissolved in
  15ml/1 tbsp boiling water (optional)
salt and ground black pepper
natural (plain) yogurt and naan
  bread, to serve

1 Chop one of the onions, then heat the oil in a large pan and fry the onion until golden brown. Add the turmeric, split peas and water, bring to the boil, then reduce the heat and simmer for 20 minutes.

COOK'S TIP
Fresh spinach is also delicious in this soup. Add 50g/2oz finely chopped spinach leaves to the soup with the parsley, coriander and chives.

2 Meanwhile, grate the other onion into a bowl, add the minced beef and seasoning and mix. Using your hands, form the mixture into small balls, about the size of walnuts. Carefully add to the pan and simmer for 10 minutes.

3 Add the rice, then stir in the chopped parsley, coriander and chives and simmer for about 30 minutes, until the rice is tender, stirring frequently.

4 Melt the butter in a small pan and gently fry the garlic. Add the chopped mint, stir briefly, and then sprinkle the mixture over the soup with the saffron liquid, if using. Serve the soup with yogurt and naan bread.

Energy 338Kcal/1409kJ; Protein 14.8g; Carbohydrate 42g, of which sugars 5.3g; Fat 12.5g, of which saturates 4.5g; Cholesterol 28mg; Calcium 64mg; Fibre 2.5g; Sodium 57mg.

SPINACH AND LEMON SOUP WITH MEATBALLS

THIS SOUP — OR A VARIATION OF IT — IS STANDARD FARE THROUGHOUT THE MIDDLE EAST. IN TURKEY, WITHOUT MEATBALLS, IT IS POPULARLY REFERRED TO AS WEDDING SOUP.

SERVES SIX

INGREDIENTS
2 large onions
45ml/3 tbsp oil
15ml/1 tbsp ground turmeric
90g/3½oz/½ cup yellow split peas
1.2 litres/2 pints/5 cups water
225g/8oz minced (ground) lamb
450g/1lb spinach, chopped
50g/2oz/½ cup rice flour
juice of 2 lemons
1–2 garlic cloves, very finely chopped
30ml/2 tbsp chopped fresh mint
4 eggs, beaten
salt and ground black pepper

1 Chop one of the onions, heat 30ml/ 2 tbsp of the oil in a large frying pan and fry the onion until golden. Add the turmeric, split peas and water, bring to the boil then simmer for 20 minutes.

2 Grate the remaining onion into a bowl, add the minced lamb and seasoning and mix. With your hands, form into small balls, about the size of walnuts. Carefully add to the pan and simmer for 10 minutes, then add the spinach, cover and simmer for 20 minutes.

3 Mix the rice flour with about 250ml/ 8fl oz/1 cup cold water to make a smooth paste, then slowly add to the pan, stirring all the time to prevent lumps. Stir in the lemon juice, season with salt and pepper and cook over a gentle heat for 20 minutes.

4 Meanwhile, heat the remaining oil in a small pan and fry the garlic briefly until golden. Stir in the chopped mint and remove the pan from the heat.

COOK'S TIP
If preferred, use less lemon juice to begin with and then add more to taste once the soup is cooked. Use minced beef or pork in place of minced lamb.

5 Remove the soup from the heat and stir in the beaten eggs. Ladle the soup into warmed soup bowls. Sprinkle the garlic and mint garnish over the soup and serve.

Energy 293Kcal/1222kJ; Protein 18.3g; Carbohydrate 21.6g, of which sugars 5.2g; Fat 15.2g, of which saturates 4.3g; Cholesterol 156mg; Calcium 179mg; Fibre 3.4g; Sodium 185mg.

FALAFEL

THESE TASTY DEEP-FRIED PATTIES ARE ONE OF THE NATIONAL DISHES OF EGYPT AND ARE ALSO POPULAR IN ISRAEL AND OTHER MIDDLE EASTERN COUNTRIES. THEY MAKE AN EXCELLENT APPETIZER.

SERVES SIX

INGREDIENTS

450g/1lb/2½ cups dried white beans
2 red onions, chopped
2 large garlic cloves, crushed
45ml/3 tbsp finely chopped
  fresh parsley
5ml/1 tsp ground coriander
5ml/1 tsp ground cumin
7.5ml/1½ tsp baking powder
vegetable oil, for deep frying
salt and ground black pepper
tomato salad, to serve

1 Soak the white beans overnight in water. Remove the skins and process in a blender or food processor. Add the chopped onions, garlic, chopped parsley, coriander, cumin, baking powder and seasoning and blend again to make a very smooth paste. Allow the mixture to stand at room temperature for at least 30 minutes.

2 Take walnut-size pieces of the mixture and flatten into small patties. Set aside again for about 15 minutes.

3 Heat the oil in a deep, heavy pan until it is very hot and then deep-fry the patties in batches until golden brown. Drain on kitchen paper and then serve hot with a tomato salad.

HUMMUS

THIS POPULAR MIDDLE EASTERN DIP IS WIDELY AVAILABLE IN SUPERMARKETS, BUT NOTHING COMPARES TO THE FLAVOUR OF THE HOME-MADE VARIETY. IT IS VERY EASY TO PREPARE.

SERVES FOUR TO SIX

INGREDIENTS

175g/6oz/1 cup cooked chickpeas
120ml/4fl oz/½ cup tahini paste
3 garlic cloves
juice of 2 lemons
45–60ml/3–4 tbsp water
salt and ground black pepper
fresh radishes, to serve
For the garnish
15ml/1 tbsp olive oil
15ml/1 tbsp finely chopped
  fresh parsley
2.5ml/½ tsp paprika
4 pitted black olives

1 Place the chickpeas, tahini paste, garlic, lemon juice, seasoning and a little of the water in a blender or food processor. Process until smooth, adding a little more water, if necessary.

2 Alternatively, if you don't have a blender or food processor, mash the ingredients together in a small bowl until smooth in consistency.

3 Spoon the mixture into a shallow dish. Make a dent in the middle and pour the olive oil garnish into it. Garnish with chopped parsley, paprika and olives and serve with the radishes.

COOK'S TIP
Canned chickpeas can be used for hummus. Drain and rinse under cold water before processing.

TOP Energy 409Kcal/1704kJ; Protein 16.9g; Carbohydrate 22.2g, of which sugars 1.5g; Fat 28.7g, of which saturates 4g; Cholesterol 0mg; Calcium 350mg; Fibre 8.1g; Sodium 26mg.
BOTTOM Energy 303Kcal/1282kJ; Protein 18.5g; Carbohydrate 44.7g, of which sugars 5.2g; Fat 6.9g, of which saturates 1.2g; Cholesterol 0mg; Calcium 88mg; Fibre 7.2g; Sodium 16mg.

TABBOULEH

THE BULGUR WHEAT THAT GIVES THIS CLASSIC ARAB SALAD ITS DELICIOUS NUTTINESS IS NOT COOKED, JUST SOAKED IN COLD WATER. TOMATOES, FRESH HERBS AND LEMON JUICE ADD TO THE FLAVOUR.

SERVES FOUR

INGREDIENTS
175g/6oz/1 cup fine bulgur wheat
juice of 1 lemon
45ml/3 tbsp olive oil
40g/1½oz fresh parsley,
    finely chopped
45ml/3 tbsp fresh mint, chopped
4–5 spring onions (scallions),
    chopped
1 green (bell) pepper, seeded
    and sliced
salt and ground black pepper
2 large tomatoes, diced, and pitted
    black olives, to garnish

1 Put the bulgur wheat in a bowl. Add enough cold water to cover the wheat and let it stand for at least 30 minutes and up to 2 hours.

2 Drain and squeeze with your hands to remove excess water. The bulgur wheat will swell to double the size. Spread on kitchen paper to dry the bulgur wheat completely.

3 Place the bulgur wheat in a large bowl, add the lemon juice, the oil and a little salt and pepper. Allow to stand for 1–2 hours if possible, in order for the flavours to develop.

4 Add the chopped parsley, chopped mint, spring onions and pepper and mix well. Garnish with diced tomatoes and olives and serve.

CAÇIK

TRAVELLERS THROUGHOUT THE MIDDLE EAST KNOW THIS SIMPLE DISH. IT CAN BE SERVED WITH FLAT BREAD, AS AN APPETIZER, OR AS AN ACCOMPANIMENT TO A SPICY STEW OR CURRY.

SERVES FOUR

INGREDIENTS
½ cucumber
1 small onion
2 garlic cloves
10g/¼oz fresh parsley
475ml/16fl oz/2 cups natural
    (plain) yogurt
1.5ml/¼ tsp paprika
salt and white pepper
fresh mint leaves, to garnish

1 Finely chop the cucumber and onion, crush the garlic and finely chop the parsley.

COOK'S TIP
It's not traditional, but other herbs, such as mint or chives used in place of parsley, would be equally good in this dish.

2 Lightly beat the yogurt in a bowl and then add the cucumber, onion, garlic and parsley and season with salt and pepper to taste.

3 Sprinkle with a little paprika and chill for at least 1 hour. Garnish with mint leaves and serve with warm pitta bread or as an accompaniment to meat, poultry and rice dishes.

TOP Energy 199Kcal/828kJ; Protein 3.9g; Carbohydrate 26.5g, of which sugars 3.9g; Fat 9.2g, of which saturates 1.3g; Cholesterol 0mg; Calcium 41mg; Fibre 2.1g; Sodium 13mg.
BOTTOM Energy 77Kcal/321kJ; Protein 6.6g; Carbohydrate 10.7g, of which sugars 10.3g; Fat 1.3g, of which saturates 0.6g; Cholesterol 2mg; Calcium 241mg; Fibre 0.6g; Sodium 101mg.

DOLMEH

THE WORD DOLMEH MEANS "STUFFED" IN PERSIAN, AND GENERALLY REFERS TO ANY VEGETABLE FILLED WITH RICE, HERBS, AND SOMETIMES MEAT.

SERVES FOUR TO SIX

INGREDIENTS

250g/9oz vine leaves
30ml/2 tbsp olive oil
1 large onion, finely chopped
250g/9oz minced (ground) lamb
50g/2oz/¼ cup yellow split peas
75g/3oz/½ cup cooked rice
30ml/2 tbsp chopped fresh parsley
30ml/2 tbsp chopped fresh mint
30ml/2 tbsp chopped fresh chives
3–4 spring onions (scallions),
  finely chopped
juice of 2 lemons
30ml/2 tbsp tomato purée (paste)
30ml/2 tbsp sugar
salt and ground black pepper
yogurt and pitta bread, to serve

1 Blanch fresh vine leaves if using, in boiling water for 1–2 minutes to soften them, or rinse preserved, bottled or canned vine leaves under cold water.

2 Heat the olive oil in a large frying pan and fry the onion for a few minutes until slightly softened. Add the minced lamb and fry over a medium heat until well browned, stirring frequently. Season with salt and pepper.

3 Place the split peas in a small pan with enough water to cover and bring to the boil. Cover the pan and simmer gently over a low heat for 12–15 minutes, until soft. Drain the split peas if necessary.

4 Stir the split peas, cooked rice, chopped herbs, spring onions, and the juice of one of the lemons into the meat. Add the tomato purée and then knead until thoroughly blended.

5 Place each vine leaf on a chopping board with the vein side up. Place 15ml/1 tbsp of the meat mixture on the leaf and fold the stem end over the meat. Fold the sides in towards the centre and then fold into a neat parcel.

6 Line the base of a large pan with unstuffed leaves and arrange the rolled leaves in layers on top. Stir the remaining lemon juice and sugar into 150ml/¼ pint/⅔ cup water and pour over the leaves. Place a heatproof plate over the dolmeh to keep them in shape.

7 Cover the pan and cook over a very low heat for 2 hours, checking occasionally and adding extra water if necessary. Serve with yogurt and bread.

COOK'S TIP
If using preserved vine leaves, soak them overnight in cold water and then rinse several times before use.

Energy 319Kcal/1336kJ; Protein 18.4g; Carbohydrate 29.8g, of which sugars 16.2g; Fat 14.8g, of which saturates 4.8g; Cholesterol 48mg; Calcium 117mg; Fibre 4.2g; Sodium 98mg.

BABA GANOUSH

LEGEND HAS IT THAT THIS FAMOUS MIDDLE EASTERN APPETIZER WAS INVENTED BY THE LADIES OF THE SULTAN'S HAREM WHO VIED WITH ONE ANOTHER TO WIN HIS FAVOUR.

SERVES FOUR TO SIX

INGREDIENTS

  3 aubergines (eggplants)
  2 garlic cloves, crushed
  60ml/4 tbsp tahini paste
  juice of 2 lemons
  15ml/1 tbsp paprika, plus extra
    for garnishing
  salt and ground black pepper
  chopped fresh parsley, olive oil,
    plus a few green or black olives,
    to garnish
  pitta bread or vegetable crudités,
    to serve

1 Preheat the oven to 190°C/375°F/ Gas 5. Slit the skins of the aubergines, place on a baking sheet and bake in the oven for 30–40 minutes, until the skins begin to split.

2 Place the aubergines on a chopping board and cool slightly. Carefully peel away the skins from the aubergines.

COOK'S TIP
Tahini paste can be obtained from health food shops, delicatessens and many supermarkets.

3 Place the aubergine flesh in a blender or food processor. Add the garlic, tahini paste, lemon juice, paprika and salt and pepper. Process to a smooth paste, adding about 15–30ml/1–2 tbsp water if the paste is too thick.

4 Spoon into a dish and make a dip in the centre. Garnish with extra paprika, chopped parsley, a drizzle of olive oil and olives. Serve with hot pitta bread or a selection of vegetable crudités.

Energy 159Kcal/662kJ; Protein 5.5g; Carbohydrate 3.6g, of which sugars 3.2g; Fat 13.9g, of which saturates 2.1g; Cholesterol 0mg; Calcium 168mg; Fibre 4.8g; Sodium 8mg.

BÖREKS

THE TWO CHEESE FILLING IS A FAVOURITE COMBINATION, INEVITABLY ENLIVENED WITH FRESH HERBS AND JUST A PINCH OF NUTMEG. BÖREKS ARE MORE OFTEN BAKED THAN FRIED.

MAKES THIRTY-FIVE TO FORTY

INGREDIENTS
    225g/8oz feta cheese, grated
    225g/8oz mozzarella, grated
    2 eggs, beaten
    45ml/3 tbsp chopped
        fresh parsley
    45ml/3 tbsp chopped
        fresh chives
    45ml/3 tbsp chopped
        fresh mint
    pinch of freshly grated nutmeg
    225g/8oz filo pastry sheets
    45–60ml/3–4 tbsp melted butter
    ground black pepper

1 Preheat the oven to 180°C/350°F/ Gas 4. In a bowl, blend the feta and mozzarella cheeses with the beaten eggs. Add the chopped herbs, black pepper and nutmeg, and mix well.

2 Cut the sheets of pastry into four rectangular strips approximately 7.5cm/ 3in wide. Cover all but one or two strips of the pastry with a damp cloth to prevent them from drying out.

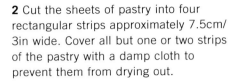

3 Brush one strip of pastry at a time with a little melted butter.

4 Place 5ml/1 tsp of filling at the bottom edge. Fold one corner over the filling to make a triangle shape. Continue folding the pastry over itself until you get to the end of the strip. Keep making triangles until all the filling is used up.

5 Place the böreks on a greased baking sheet and bake in the oven for about 30 minutes, until golden brown and crisp. Serve warm or cold.

COOK'S TIPS
A mixture of almost any cheeses can be used but avoid cream cheeses. Use chopped fresh basil in place of mint.

Energy 64Kcal/269kJ; Protein 3.1g; Carbohydrate 4.1g, of which sugars 0.2g; Fat 4.1g, of which saturates 2.5g; Cholesterol 22mg; Calcium 61mg; Fibre 0.3g; Sodium 131mg.

STUFFED PEPPERS

OF ALL THE DOLMEH, OR STUFFED VEGETABLES, THIS IS PERHAPS THE MOST COLOURFUL, ESPECIALLY WHEN MIXED COLOURS ARE USED. TRY TO FIND PEPPERS THAT ARE MORE OR LESS THE SAME SIZE.

SERVES SIX

INGREDIENTS

6 mixed (bell) peppers, red, yellow and green
30ml/2 tbsp olive oil
1 large onion, finely chopped
3–4 spring onions (scallions), finely chopped
250g/9oz minced (ground) lamb
2 garlic cloves, crushed (optional)
50g/2oz/¼ cup yellow split peas
75g/3oz/½ cup cooked rice
30ml/2 tbsp finely chopped fresh parsley
30ml/2 tbsp finely chopped fresh mint
30ml/2 tbsp finely chopped fresh chives
5ml/1 tsp ground cinnamon
juice of 2 lemons
30ml/2 tbsp tomato purée (paste)
400g/14oz can chopped tomatoes
knob of butter
salt and ground black pepper
natural (plain) yogurt and pitta bread or naan bread, to serve

1 Cut off the mixed pepper tops and set aside. Remove the seeds and cores and trim the bases so they stand squarely. Cook in salted boiling water for 5 minutes, then drain, rinse under cold water and set aside.

2 Heat the oil in a large pan or flameproof casserole and fry the onion and spring onions for about 4–5 minutes until golden brown. Add the minced lamb and fry over a medium heat until well browned, stirring frequently. Stir in the garlic if using.

3 Meanwhile, place the split peas in a small pan with enough water to cover, bring to the boil and then simmer gently for 12–15 minutes until soft. Drain.

4 Stir the split peas, cooked rice, chopped herbs, cinnamon, juice of one of the lemons, and tomato purée into the meat. Season and stir until combined.

5 Spoon the rice and split pea mixture into the peppers and place the reserved lids on top.

6 Pour the chopped tomatoes into a large pan or flameproof casserole and add the remaining lemon juice and butter. Arrange the peppers neatly in the pan with the stems upwards. Bring to the boil and then cover tightly and cook over a low heat for 40–45 minutes, until the peppers are tender.

7 Serve the peppers with the tomato sauce accompanied by yogurt and warm pitta bread or naan bread.

COOK'S TIP
Make sure that the pan or casserole that you choose is just large enough so that the peppers fit quite snugly.

Energy 267Kcal/1115kJ; Protein 13.9g; Carbohydrate 26.1g, of which sugars 15.3g; Fat 12.5g, of which saturates 4.7g; Cholesterol 37mg; Calcium 81mg; Fibre 4.4g; Sodium 84mg.

BYESAR

THE ARAB DISH BYESAR IS SIMILAR TO MIDDLE EASTERN HUMMUS, BUT USES BROAD BEANS INSTEAD OF CHICKPEAS. SERVE WITH BREAD TO SCOOP UP THE PURÉE.

SERVES FOUR TO SIX

INGREDIENTS
  115g/4oz dried broad (fava)
    beans, soaked overnight
  2 garlic cloves, peeled
  5ml/1 tsp cumin seeds
  about 60ml/4 tbsp olive oil
  salt
  fresh mint sprigs, to garnish
  extra cumin seeds, cayenne pepper
    and bread, to serve

VARIATION
Use dried chickpeas in place of broad beans if you prefer.

1 Put the dried broad beans in a pan with the whole garlic cloves and cumin seeds and add enough water just to cover. Bring to the boil, then reduce the heat, cover and simmer until the beans are tender. Drain, cool and then slip off the outer skin of each bean.

2 Process the beans in a blender or food processor, adding sufficient olive oil and water to give a smooth soft dip. Season to taste with plenty of salt. Garnish with sprigs of mint and serve with extra cumin seeds, cayenne pepper and bread.

Energy 113Kcal/468kJ; Protein 1g; Carbohydrate 2.3g, of which sugars 0.2g; Fat 11.2g, of which saturates 1.6g; Cholesterol 0mg; Calcium 7mg; Fibre 0.5g; Sodium 2mg.

BASTELA WITH GINGER AND CASHEW NUTS

IN THIS SIMPLIFIED VERSION, GROUND CASHEWS ARE USED IN PLACE OF THE MORE COMMON ALMONDS, AND GINGER, CORIANDER AND CINNAMON PROVIDE THE WARM SPICE NOTES.

SERVES SIX

INGREDIENTS
    30ml/2 tbsp olive oil
    115g/4oz/½ cup butter
    8 spring onions (scallions), trimmed
      and chopped
    2 garlic cloves, chopped
    25g/1oz fresh root ginger, peeled
      and chopped
    225g/8oz/1⅓ cups cashew nuts,
      roughly chopped
    5–10ml/1–2 tsp ground cinnamon,
      plus extra to garnish
    5ml/1 tsp paprika
    2.5ml/½ tsp ground coriander
    6 eggs, beaten
    bunch of fresh flat leaf parsley,
      finely chopped
    large bunch of fresh coriander
      (cilantro), finely chopped
    8 sheets of ouarka or filo pastry
    salt and ground black pepper

1 Preheat the oven to 200°C/400°F/ Gas 6. Heat the olive oil with a little of the butter in a heavy pan and stir in the spring onions, garlic and ginger. Add the cashew nuts and cook for a few minutes, then stir in the cinnamon, paprika and ground coriander.

2 Season the mixture well, then add the beaten eggs. Cook, stirring constantly, until the eggs begin to scramble but remain moist. Remove the pan from the heat, add the chopped parsley and fresh coriander, and leave to cool.

VARIATION
Instead of making a single large pie, you can make small, individual pies for a picnic or to serve with drinks at a party. Simply cut the filo into strips or triangles, add a spoonful of the filling and fold them up into tight little parcels, making sure the edges are well sealed.

3 Melt the remaining butter. Separate the sheets of ouarka or filo and keep them under a slightly damp cloth. Brush the base of an ovenproof dish with a little of the melted butter and cover with a sheet of pastry, allowing the sides to flop over the rim.

4 Brush the pastry with a little more of the melted butter and place another sheet of pastry on top of the first. Repeat with another two sheets of pastry to make four layers.

5 Spread the cashew nut mixture on the pastry and fold the pastry edges over the filling. Cover with the remaining sheets of pastry, brushing each one with melted butter and tucking the edges under the pie, as though making a bed.

6 Brush the top of the pie with the remaining melted butter and bake for 25 minutes, until the pastry is crisp and golden. Dust the top of the pie with a little extra ground cinnamon and then serve immediately.

Energy 528Kcal/2190kJ; Protein 15.9g; Carbohydrate 17.6g, of which sugars 3.1g; Fat 44.5g, of which saturates 15.9g; Cholesterol 231mg; Calcium 93mg; Fibre 2.4g; Sodium 300mg.

SIZZLING PRAWNS

IN COASTAL REGIONS OF THE MIDDLE EAST, STREET FOOD OFTEN MEANS A MAN WITH A PAN COOKING SPICY SEAFOOD OVER A SMALL BRAZIER. PRAWNS COOKED THIS WAY TASTE GREAT.

SERVES FOUR

INGREDIENTS
    450g/1lb raw king prawns (jumbo
      shrimp) in their shells
    30ml/2 tbsp olive oil
    25–40g/1–1½oz/2–3 tbsp butter
    2 garlic cloves, crushed
    5ml/1 tsp ground cumin
    2.5ml/½ tsp ground ginger
    10ml/2 tsp paprika
    1.5ml/¼ tsp cayenne pepper
    lemon wedges and fresh coriander
      (cilantro) sprigs, to garnish

1 Pull the heads off the prawns and then peel away and discard the shells, legs and tails. Using a sharp knife, cut along the back of each prawn and pull away and discard the dark thread.

2 Heat the olive oil and butter in a frying pan. When the butter begins to sizzle, add the garlic and cook for about 30 seconds.

3 Add the cumin, ginger, paprika and cayenne pepper. Cook briefly, stirring for a few seconds, and then add the prawns. Cook for 2–3 minutes over a high heat, until they turn pink, stirring frequently.

4 Transfer the prawns to four warmed serving dishes and pour the butter and spicy mixture over. Garnish with lemon wedges and coriander and serve.

GRILLED KEFTAS

CLOSELY RELATED TO THE KOFTAS OF INDIA AND THE MIDDLE EAST, THESE SPICY LAMB SAUSAGE SKEWERS WITH A MINT AND YOGURT DRESSING ARE A MOROCCAN SPECIALITY.

MAKES TWELVE TO FOURTEEN

INGREDIENTS
    675g/1½lb lean lamb
    1 onion, quartered
    3–4 fresh parsley sprigs
    2–3 fresh coriander (cilantro) sprigs
    1–2 fresh mint sprigs
    2.5ml/½ tsp ground cumin
    2.5ml/½ tsp mixed spice (apple
      pie spice)
    5ml/1 tsp paprika
    salt and ground black pepper
    Moroccan bread, to serve
For the mint dressing
    30ml/2 tbsp finely chopped
      fresh mint
    90ml/6 tbsp natural (plain) yogurt

1 Roughly chop the lamb, place in a food processor and process until smooth. Transfer to a plate.

2 Add the onion, parsley, coriander and mint to the processor and process until finely chopped. Add the lamb together with the ground spices and seasoning and process again until very smooth. Transfer to a bowl and chill for about 1 hour.

3 Make the dressing. Blend the chopped mint with the yogurt and chill until required.

4 Mould the meat into small sausage shapes and skewer with wooden or metal kebab sticks. Preheat a grill (broiler) or barbecue to a medium heat.

5 Cook the keftas for 5–6 minutes, turning once. Serve immediately with the mint dressing. Moroccan bread makes a good accompaniment.

TOP Energy 182Kcal/756kJ; Protein 19.9g; Carbohydrate 0g, of which sugars 0g; Fat 11.3g, of which saturates 4.2g; Cholesterol 233mg; Calcium 90mg; Fibre 0g; Sodium 252mg.
BOTTOM Energy 111Kcal/463kJ; Protein 11.7g; Carbohydrate 1.7g, of which sugars 1.3g; Fat 6.4g, of which saturates 3g; Cholesterol 43mg; Calcium 29mg; Fibre 0.2g; Sodium 56mg.

HOT SPICY PRAWNS WITH CORIANDER

CORIANDER HAS A LONG HISTORY. NATIVE TO THE MEDITERRANEAN AND THE MIDDLE EAST, IT WAS KNOWN TO THE ANCIENT EGYPTIANS, AND SEEDS HAVE BEEN FOUND IN THE TOMBS OF THE PHARAOHS. TODAY, CORIANDER IS WIDELY GROWN, AND IT IS OFTEN USED TO FLAVOUR TAGINES AND SIMILAR DISHES. THE HERB'S AFFINITY FOR CUMIN IS WELL KNOWN, SO IT IS NOT SURPRISING TO FIND THE TWIN FLAVOURINGS USED IN THIS SPICY APPETIZER.

SERVES TWO TO FOUR

INGREDIENTS
  60ml/4 tbsp olive oil
  2–3 garlic cloves, chopped
  25g/1oz fresh root ginger, peeled
    and grated
  1 fresh red or green chilli, seeded
    and chopped
  5ml/1 tsp cumin seeds
  5ml/1 tsp paprika
  450g/1lb uncooked king prawns
    (jumbo shrimp), shelled
  bunch of fresh coriander
    (cilantro), chopped
  salt
  1 lemon, cut into wedges, to serve

1 In a large frying pan, heat the oil with the garlic. Stir in the ginger, chilli and cumin seeds. Cook briefly, until the ingredients give off a lovely aroma, then add the paprika and toss in the prawns.

2 Fry the prawns over a fairly high heat, turning them frequently, for 3–5 minutes, until just cooked. Season to taste with salt and add the coriander. Serve immediately, with lemon wedges for squeezing over the prawns.

COOK'S TIP
When buying garlic, choose plump garlic with tightly packed cloves and dry skin. Avoid any bulbs with soft, shrivelled cloves or green shoots.

Energy 382Kcal/1591kJ; Protein 40.8g; Carbohydrate 1.1g, of which sugars 0.9g; Fat 23.9g, of which saturates 3.4g; Cholesterol 439mg; Calcium 254mg; Fibre 1.9g; Sodium 440mg.

BUS-STATION KEFTA WITH EGG AND TOMATO

THE TITLE SAYS IT ALL. THIS IS THE TYPE OF SNACK THAT IS ON SALE IN BUS AND TRAIN STATIONS THROUGHOUT THE MIDDLE EAST. IT IS COOKED ON THE SPOT AND EATEN STRAIGHT FROM THE PAN. SPEED IS ESSENTIAL WHEN TRAVELLERS ARE ABOUT TO DEPART, SO THIS IS THE PERFECT DISH FOR A QUICK BRUNCH OR IMPROMPTU DINNER OR SUPPER. MAKE THE TINY MEATBALLS IN ADVANCE AND KEEP THEM CHILLED UNTIL THEY ARE NEEDED.

SERVES FOUR

INGREDIENTS
   225g/8oz minced (ground) lamb
   1 onion, finely chopped
   50g/2oz/1 cup fresh breadcrumbs
   5 eggs
   5ml/1 tsp ground cinnamon
   bunch of flat leaf parsley, chopped
   30ml/2 tbsp olive oil
   400g/14oz can chopped tomatoes
   10ml/2 tsp sugar
   5ml/1 tsp ras el hanout
   small bunch of fresh coriander
    (cilantro), roughly chopped
   salt and ground black pepper
   crusty bread, to serve

1 In a bowl, knead the minced lamb with the onion, breadcrumbs, 1 egg, cinnamon, chopped parsley and salt and pepper until well mixed. Lift the mixture in your hand and slap it down into the bowl several times.

2 Take a small amount of mixture and shape it into a small ball about the size of a walnut. Repeat with the remaining mixture to make about 12 balls.

3 Heat the olive oil in a large, heavy frying pan. Fry the meatballs until nicely browned, turning them occasionally so they cook evenly.

4 Stir the tomatoes, sugar, ras el hanout and most of the chopped coriander in to the pan. Bring to the boil, cook for a few minutes to reduce the liquid, and roll the balls round in the sauce. Season to taste with salt and pepper.

5 Make room for the remaining eggs in the pan and crack them into spaces between the meatballs. Cover the pan, reduce the heat and cook for about 3 minutes or until the eggs are just set.

6 Sprinkle with the remaining chopped coriander and serve in the pan, with chunks of bread to use as scoops.

Energy 330Kcal/1381kJ; Protein 21.5g; Carbohydrate 16.7g, of which sugars 6.6g; Fat 20.4g, of which saturates 6.2g; Cholesterol 281mg; Calcium 97mg; Fibre 1.7g; Sodium 264mg

FISH

Harvesting the riches of rivers and the sea has always been an important activity for the people of the Middle East. The daily catch is sold as soon as the boats return to shore, to be cooked the same day, or preserved by drying, salting or pickling. Arabs have a vast store of fish recipes, but often prefer the simplest methods of cooking, like grilling over an open fire.

SYRIAN BAKED FISH WITH TAHINI

TAHINI IS A SESAME SEED PASTE THAT IS POPULAR THROUGHOUT THE ARAB COUNTRIES IN BOTH SWEET AND SAVOURY DISHES. MOST PEOPLE KNOW IT AS AN INGREDIENT IN AUTHENTIC HUMMUS, BUT IT IS ALSO VERY GOOD WITH FISH. THIS RECIPE COMES FROM TARTOUS, A FISHING TOWN ON SYRIA'S MEDITERRANEAN COASTLINE.

SERVES SIX

INGREDIENTS
6 cod or haddock fillets
juice of 2 lemons
60ml/4 tbsp olive oil
2 large onions, chopped
250ml/8fl oz/1 cup tahini paste
1 garlic clove, crushed
45–60ml/3–4 tbsp water
salt and ground black pepper
boiled rice and a green salad,
   to serve

1 Preheat the oven to 180°C/350°F/Gas 4. Arrange the fish fillets in a shallow ovenproof dish, pour over 15ml/1 tbsp each of the lemon juice and olive oil and bake for 20 minutes.

2 Meanwhile heat the remaining oil in a large frying pan and fry the onions for 6–8 minutes, until well browned and almost crisp.

3 Put the tahini paste, garlic and seasoning in a small bowl and slowly beat in the remaining lemon juice and water, a little at a time, until the sauce is light and creamy.

4 Sprinkle the onions over the fish, pour over the tahini sauce and bake for a further 15 minutes, until the fish is cooked through and the sauce is bubbling. Serve the fish at once with boiled rice and a salad.

Energy 434Kcal/1800kJ; Protein 33.8g; Carbohydrate 0.7g, of which sugars 0.2g; Fat 32.9g, of which saturates 4.7g; Cholesterol 65mg; Calcium 296mg; Fibre 3.4g; Sodium 93mg.

EGYPTIAN BAKED FISH WITH NUTS

THE ARABIC WORD FOR RED MULLET IS SULTAN IBRAHIM. IT IS A VERY POPULAR FISH IN THE MIDDLE EAST AND IS OFTEN SERVED WHOLE IN THE FISH RESTAURANTS OF ALEXANDRIA AND ABU QIR ON EGYPT'S NORTH COAST. THE SAUCE FOR THIS DISH IS MADE WITH CHOPPED HAZELNUTS AND PINE NUTS, WHICH NOT ONLY ADD FLAVOUR, BUT ALSO THICKEN THE TOMATO AND HERB MIXTURE.

SERVES FOUR

INGREDIENTS
    45ml/3 tbsp sunflower oil
    4 small red mullet or snapper, gutted
      and cleaned
    1 large onion, finely chopped
    75g/3oz/½ cup hazelnuts, chopped
    75g/3oz/½ cup pine nuts
    3–4 tomatoes, sliced
    45–60ml/3–4 tbsp finely chopped
      fresh parsley
    250ml/8fl oz/1 cup fish stock
    salt and ground black pepper
    fresh parsley sprigs, to garnish
    cooked new potatoes or rice, and
      vegetables or salad, to serve

1 Preheat the oven to 190°C/375°F/ Gas 5. Heat 30ml/2 tbsp of the oil in a frying pan and fry the fish, two at a time, until crisp on both sides.

2 Meanwhile, heat the remaining oil in a large pan or flameproof casserole and fry the onion for 3–4 minutes, until golden. Add the chopped hazelnuts and pine nuts and stir-fry for a few minutes.

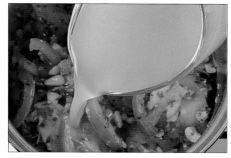

3 Stir in the tomatoes, cook for a few minutes and then add the chopped parsley, seasoning and stock and simmer for 10–15 minutes, stirring occasionally.

4 Place the fish in an ovenproof dish and spoon the sauce over. Bake in the oven for 20 minutes, until the fish is cooked through and flakes easily when tested with a knife.

5 Serve the fish immediately, accompanied by cooked new potatoes or rice, and vegetables or salad.

VARIATION
Other small whole fish, such as snapper or trout, can be used for this recipe if mullet is unavailable.

Energy 470Kcal/1952kJ; Protein 25.8g; Carbohydrate 10.4g, of which sugars 8.3g; Fat 36.4g, of which saturates 2.9g; Cholesterol 0mg; Calcium 166mg; Fibre 4.9g; Sodium 108mg.

LEBANESE FISH WITH RICE

THIS IS A FINE EXAMPLE OF SAADIYEH, WHICH MEANS A PLAIN FISH DISH WITH RICE. IT IS IMPORTANT TO USE A GOOD QUALITY FISH STOCK, PREFERABLY ONE WHICH YOU HAVE MADE YOURSELF.

SERVES FOUR TO SIX

INGREDIENTS
  juice of 1 lemon
  45ml/3 tbsp olive oil
  900g/2lb cod steaks
  4 large onions, chopped
  5ml/1 tsp ground cumin
  2–3 saffron threads
  1 litre/1¾ pints/4 cups fish stock
  450g/1lb/2¼ cups basmati or other
    long grain rice
  50g/2oz/⅓ cup pine nuts,
    lightly toasted
  salt and ground black pepper
  fresh flat leaf parsley sprigs,
    to garnish

1 Whisk together the lemon juice and 15ml/1 tbsp of the oil in a shallow, non-metallic dish. Add the fish, turn to coat well, then cover and leave to marinate for 30 minutes.

2 Heat the remaining oil in a large pan or flameproof casserole and fry the onions for 5–6 minutes, until golden, stirring occasionally.

COOK'S TIP
Take care when cooking the rice that the pan does not boil dry. Check it occasionally and add more stock or water if it becomes necessary.

3 Drain the fish, reserving the marinade, and add to the pan. Fry for 1–2 minutes each side until golden, then add the cumin and saffron.

4 Pour in the fish stock, the reserved marinade and a little salt and pepper. Bring to the boil and then simmer very gently over a low heat for 5–10 minutes, until the fish is nearly done.

5 Transfer the fish to a plate and keep warm, then add the rice to the stock. Bring to the boil and then reduce the heat and simmer very gently for 15 minutes, until nearly all the stock has been absorbed.

6 Arrange the fish over the rice and cover the pan. Cook over a low heat for a further 15–20 minutes.

7 Transfer the fish to a plate, then spoon the rice on to a large, warmed, flat dish and arrange the fish steaks on top.

8 Sprinkle the fish with toasted pine nuts and garnish with parsley sprigs. Serve immediately.

Energy 834Kcal/3483kJ; Protein 54.3g; Carbohydrate 110g, of which sugars 14.5g; Fat 19.5g, of which saturates 2g; Cholesterol 104mg; Calcium 106mg; Fibre 3.7g; Sodium 143mg.

TURKISH COLD FISH

WHOLE FISH, COOKED IN A FLAVOURSOME SAUCE AND SERVED COLD, OFTEN FORM THE CENTREPIECE
OF A MIDDLE EASTERN MEAL. THIS VERSION FROM TURKEY CAN ALSO BE MADE USING MACKEREL.

SERVES FOUR

INGREDIENTS
   60ml/4 tbsp olive oil
   900g/2lb red mullet or snapper
   2 onions, sliced
   1 green (bell) pepper, seeded
    and sliced
   1 red (bell) pepper, seeded and sliced
   3 garlic cloves, crushed
   15ml/1 tbsp tomato purée (paste)
   50ml/2fl oz/¼ cup fish stock
    or water
   5–6 tomatoes, skinned and sliced or
    400g/14oz can chopped tomatoes
   30ml/2 tbsp chopped fresh parsley
   30ml/2 tbsp lemon juice
   5ml/1 tsp paprika
   15–20 green and black olives
   salt and ground black pepper
   fresh bread and salad, to serve

1 Heat 30ml/2 tbsp of the oil in a large, flameproof roasting pan or frying pan and fry the fish on both sides, until golden brown. Remove from the pan, cover and keep warm.

2 Heat the remaining oil in the roasting pan or frying pan and fry the onions for 2–3 minutes, until slightly softened. Add the sliced peppers and continue cooking for 3–4 minutes, then add the garlic and stir-fry for a further minute.

3 Blend the tomato purée with the fish stock or water and stir into the pan with the tomatoes, chopped parsley, lemon juice, paprika and seasoning. Simmer gently without boiling for 15 minutes, stirring occasionally.

4 Return the fish to the roasting pan or frying pan and cover with the sauce. Cook for 10 minutes, then add the olives and cook for a further 5 minutes, until just cooked through.

5 Transfer the fish to a serving dish and pour the sauce over the top. Allow to cool, then cover and chill until completely cold. Serve cold with bread and salad.

VARIATION
One large fish looks spectacular, but it is tricky to both cook and serve. If you prefer, buy four smaller fish and cook for a shorter time, until just tender and cooked through but not overdone.

Energy 352Kcal/1466kJ; Protein 25g; Carbohydrate 15.8g, of which sugars 13.7g; Fat 21.5g, of which saturates 2.5g; Cholesterol 0mg; Calcium 158mg; Fibre 5.3g; Sodium 1124mg.

TILAPIA IN MANGO AND TOMATO SAUCE

THE FLESH OF TILAPIA IS WHITE AND MOIST, WITH A SWEET FLAVOUR THAT IS ACCENTUATED WHEN IT IS COOKED WITH FRUIT, AS HERE. THE FISH IS POPULAR IN ISRAEL AND LEBANON.

SERVES FOUR

INGREDIENTS

4 tilapia
juice of ½ lemon
2 garlic cloves, crushed
2.5ml/½ tsp dried thyme
30ml/2 tbsp chopped spring onion
  (scallion)
vegetable oil, for shallow frying
plain (all-purpose) flour, for dusting
30ml/2 tbsp groundnut (peanut) oil
15g/½oz/1 tbsp butter or margarine
1 onion, finely chopped
3 tomatoes, skinned and
  finely chopped
5ml/1 tsp ground turmeric
60ml/4 tbsp white wine
1 fresh green chilli, seeded and
  finely chopped
600ml/1 pint/2½ cups well-flavoured
  fish stock
5ml/1 tsp sugar
1 under-ripe medium mango, peeled,
  stoned (pitted) and diced
15ml/1 tbsp chopped fresh parsley
salt and ground black pepper

1 Place the fish in a shallow bowl, drizzle the lemon juice all over the fish and gently rub in the garlic, thyme and some salt and pepper.

2 Place some of the spring onion in the cavity of each fish, cover loosely with clear film (plastic wrap) and leave to marinate for a few hours or overnight in the refrigerator.

3 Heat a little vegetable oil in a large frying pan, coat the fish with some flour, and then fry the fish on both sides for a few minutes, until golden brown. Remove with a slotted spoon to a plate and set aside.

4 Heat the groundnut oil and butter or margarine in a pan and fry the onion for 4–5 minutes, until soft. Stir in the tomatoes and cook briskly for a few minutes.

5 Add the turmeric, white wine, chilli, fish stock and sugar and stir well. Bring to the boil, then simmer gently, covered, for 10 minutes. Add the fish and cook for about 15–20 minutes.

6 Add the mango, arranging it around the fish, and cook briefly for 1–2 minutes to heat through.

7 Arrange the fish on a warmed serving plate with the mango and tomato sauce poured over. Garnish with chopped parsley and serve immediately.

Energy 238Kcal/998kJ; Protein 23.4g; Carbohydrate 10.1g, of which sugars 9.6g; Fat 10.8g, of which saturates 3.1g; Cholesterol 8mg; Calcium 168mg; Fibre 2g; Sodium 97mg.

BAKED RED SNAPPER

A RECIPE DOESN'T HAVE TO BE ELABORATE TO TASTE GOOD. THIS COULDN'T BE SIMPLER, BUT THE FISH IS DELICIOUS WHEN BAKED WHOLE WITH ITS LIGHTLY SPICED TOMATO SAUCE.

SERVES THREE TO FOUR

INGREDIENTS
1 large red snapper, cleaned
juice of 1 lemon
2.5ml/½ tsp paprika
2.5ml/½ tsp garlic powder
2.5ml/½ tsp dried thyme
2.5ml/½ tsp ground black pepper
For the sauce
30ml/2 tbsp palm or vegetable oil
1 onion, peeled and chopped
400g/14oz can chopped tomatoes
2 garlic cloves
1 fresh thyme sprig or 2.5ml/½ tsp
  dried thyme
1 fresh green chilli, seeded and
  finely chopped
½ green (bell) pepper, seeded
  and chopped
300ml/½ pint/1¼ cups fish stock

1 Preheat the oven to 200°C/400°F/ Gas 6 and then prepare the sauce. Heat the oil in a pan, fry the onion for 5 minutes, and then add the tomatoes, garlic, thyme and chilli.

2 Add the green pepper and stock. Bring to the boil, stirring, then reduce the heat and simmer, covered, for about 10 minutes, until the vegetables are soft. Remove from the heat and cool slightly and then place in a blender or food processor and process to form a purée.

COOK'S TIP
If you prefer less sauce, remove the foil after 20 minutes and continue baking uncovered, until cooked.

3 Wash the fish well and then score the skin with a sharp knife in a criss-cross pattern. Mix together the lemon juice, paprika, garlic, thyme and black pepper, spoon over the fish and rub in well.

4 Place the fish in a greased baking dish and pour the sauce over the top. Cover with foil and bake for about 30–40 minutes, until the fish is cooked and flakes easily when tested with a knife. Serve with boiled rice.

Energy 198Kcal/837kJ; Protein 33.1g; Carbohydrate 7.4g, of which sugars 6.6g; Fat 4.3g, of which saturates 0.8g; Cholesterol 58mg; Calcium 91mg; Fibre 1.7g; Sodium 201mg.

STUFFED SARDINES

THIS DISH DOES NOT TAKE A LOT OF PREPARATION TIME AND IT IS A MEAL IN ITSELF. JUST SERVE IT WITH A CRISP GREEN SALAD TOSSED IN A FRESH LEMON DRESSING TO MAKE IT COMPLETE.

SERVES FOUR

INGREDIENTS
    900g/2lb fresh sardines
    30ml/2 tbsp olive oil
    75g/3oz/½ cup wholemeal
      breadcrumbs
    50g/2oz/¼ cup sultanas
    50g/2oz/½ cup pine nuts
    50g/2oz canned anchovy fillets,
      drained
    60ml/4 tbsp chopped fresh parsley
    1 onion, finely chopped
    salt and freshly ground black pepper

1 Preheat the oven to 200°C/400°F/Gas 6. Gut the sardines and wipe them out thoroughly with kitchen paper. Heat about 15ml/1 tbsp of the oil in a frying pan and fry the breadcrumbs until golden brown.

2 Add the sultanas, pine nuts, drained anchovies, chopped parsley, onion and seasoning and mix well.

3 Carefully fill each of the cleaned sardines with the herb and breadcrumb stuffing. When the sardine is full, close it firmly together and place it in the bottom of an ovenproof dish.

4 As the sardines are stuffed, scatter a little of the remaining filling and drizzle a little of the remaining olive oil over them.

5 Bake the fish for 30 minutes in the preheated oven, then serve at once.

Energy 550kcal/2299kJ; Protein 42.8g; Carbohydrate 28.7g, of which sugars 13.2g; Fat 30g, of which saturates 5.6g; Cholesterol 8mg; Calcium 258mg; Fibre 1.8g; Sodium 830mg.

FISH IN VINE LEAVES WITH DIPPING SAUCE

ALMOST ANY TYPE OF FIRM WHITE FISH CAN BE USED TO MAKE THESE KEBABS. THE FISH IS FIRST MARINATED IN CHERMOULA AND THEN WRAPPED IN VINE LEAVES TO SEAL IN THE FLAVOURS.

SERVES FOUR

INGREDIENTS

about 30 preserved vine leaves
4–5 large white fish fillets, skinned,
  such as haddock, ling or monkfish
For the chermoula
small bunch of fresh coriander
  (cilantro), finely chopped
2–3 garlic cloves, chopped
5–10ml/1–2 tsp ground cumin
60ml/4 tbsp olive oil
juice of 1 lemon
salt
For the dipping sauce
50ml/2fl oz/¼ cup white wine
  vinegar or lemon juice
115g/4oz/generous ½ cup caster
  (superfine) sugar
15–30ml/1–2 tbsp water
pinch of saffron threads
1 onion, finely chopped
2 garlic cloves, finely chopped
2–3 spring onions (scallions),
  thinly sliced
25g/1oz fresh root ginger, peeled
  and grated
2 hot fresh red or green chillies,
  seeded and thinly sliced
small bunch of fresh coriander
  (cilantro), finely chopped
small bunch of mint, finely chopped

1 To make the chermoula, pound the ingredients in a mortar with a pestle, or process in a food processor.

2 Rinse the vine leaves in a bowl, then soak them in cold water. Remove any bones from the fish and cut each fillet into about eight bitesize pieces. Coat the pieces of fish in the chermoula, cover and chill for 1 hour.

3 Meanwhile, prepare the dipping sauce. Heat the vinegar or lemon juice with the sugar and water until the sugar has dissolved. Bring to the boil and boil for about 1 minute, then leave to cool. Add the remaining ingredients and mix well to combine. Spoon the sauce into small individual bowls and set aside until ready to serve.

4 Drain the vine leaves and pat dry on kitchen paper. Lay a vine leaf flat on the work surface and place a piece of marinated fish in the centre. Fold the edges of the leaf over the fish, then wrap up the fish and leaf into a small parcel. Repeat with the remaining pieces of fish and vine leaves. Thread the parcels on to kebab skewers and brush with any leftover marinade.

5 Heat the grill (broiler) on the hottest setting and cook the kebabs for 2–3 minutes on each side. Serve immediately, with the sweet and sour chilli sauce for dipping.

Energy 295Kcal/1232kJ; Protein 40.7g; Carbohydrate 3.8g, of which sugars 2.3g; Fat 13g, of which saturates 1.8g; Cholesterol 98mg; Calcium 111mg; Fibre 1.6g; Sodium 139mg.

BAKED FISH <u>WITH</u> TAHINI SAUCE

THIS SIMPLE DISH IS A GREAT FAVOURITE IN MANY ARAB COUNTRIES, PARTICULARLY EGYPT, THE LEBANON AND SYRIA. CHOOSE ANY WHOLE WHITE FISH, SUCH AS SEA BASS, HAKE, BREAM OR SNAPPER.

SERVES FOUR

INGREDIENTS
1 whole fish, about 1.1kg/2½lb,
  scaled and cleaned
10ml/2 tsp coriander seeds
4 garlic cloves, sliced
10ml/2 tsp harissa sauce
90ml/6 tbsp olive oil
6 plum tomatoes, sliced
1 mild onion, sliced
3 preserved lemons, or 1
  fresh lemon
plenty of fresh herbs, such as bay
  leaves, thyme and rosemary
salt and freshly ground
  black pepper
fresh herbs, to garnish
For the sauce
75ml/3fl oz/⅔ cup light
  tahini paste
juice of 1 lemon
1 garlic clove, crushed
45ml/3 tbsp finely chopped fresh
  parsley or coriander (cilantro)

1 Preheat the oven to 200°C/400°F/Gas 6. Grease the base and sides of a large shallow ovenproof dish or a roasting pan.

2 Slash the fish diagonally on both sides with a sharp knife. Finely crush the coriander seeds and garlic with a pestle and mortar. Mix with the harissa sauce and about 60ml/4 tbsp of the olive oil.

3 Spread a little of the harissa paste inside the cavity of the fish. Spread the rest over each side of the fish and set aside.

4 Scatter the tomato slices, onion and the preserved or fresh lemon into the dish. (Thinly slice the lemon if using a fresh one.) Sprinkle over the remaining oil and season well with salt and pepper. Lay the prepared fish on top and tuck plenty of fresh herbs around it.

5 Bake the dish in the preheated oven, uncovered, for about 25 minutes, or until the fish has turned opaque and feels tender when you pierce the thickest part with a knife.

6 Meanwhile, make the sauce. Put the tahini paste, lemon juice, garlic and parsley or coriander in a small pan with 120ml/4fl oz/½ cup water and add a little salt and pepper to taste.

7 Cook the sauce gently, stirring until it is smooth and heated through.

8 Serve it in a separate dish, with the fish on a plate, garnished with herbs.

COOK'S TIP
If you can't get a suitable large fish, use a small whole fish such as red mullet or even cod or haddock steaks. Remember to reduce the cooking time slightly.

VARIATION
For a slightly spicy version, add 1 finely chopped red chilli to the sauce, making sure you remove all the seeds first.

Energy 500Kcal/2,083kJ; Protein 43.8g; Carbohydrate 6.9g, of which sugars 6.4g; Fat 33.2g, of which saturates 4.9g; Cholesterol 160mg; Calcium 426mg; Fibre 4g; Sodium 161mg.

LAMB
AND BEEF

In the Middle East, lamb is the dominant meat, but beef is also popular. The food is often cooked over an open fire, and kebabs are universally enjoyed, such as Spicy Beef Koftas and a lamb Shish Kebab. One of the most unusual dishes featured here is Lebanese Kibbeh, in which two meat mixtures, one with bulgur wheat, are layered and baked in the oven.

PERSIAN LAMB WITH SPLIT PEAS

THIS DISH — KHORESH GHAIMEH — IS TRADITIONALLY SERVED AT PARTIES AND RELIGIOUS FESTIVALS IN IRAN. THE RECIPE IS ANCIENT, AND ORIGINALLY USED PRESERVED MEAT.

SERVES FOUR

INGREDIENTS

25g/1oz/2 tbsp butter or margarine
1 large onion, chopped
450g/1lb lean lamb, cut into
  small cubes
5ml/1 tsp ground turmeric
5ml/1 tsp ground cinnamon
5ml/1 tsp curry powder
300ml/½ pint/1¼ cups water
2–3 saffron threads
90g/3½oz/½ cup yellow split peas
3 dried limes
3–4 tomatoes, chopped
30ml/2 tbsp olive oil
2 large potatoes, diced
salt and ground black pepper
cooked rice, to serve

1 Melt the butter or margarine in a large pan or flameproof casserole and fry the onion for 3–4 minutes, until golden, stirring occasionally. Add the meat and cook over a high heat for a further 3–4 minutes, until it has browned.

2 Add the turmeric, cinnamon and curry powder and cook for about 2 minutes, stirring frequently.

3 Stir in the water, season well and bring to the boil, then cover and simmer over a low heat for about 30–35 minutes. Stir the saffron into about 15ml/1 tbsp boiling water.

4 Add the saffron liquid to the meat with the split peas, dried limes and tomatoes. Stir well and then simmer, covered, for a further 35 minutes, until the meat is completely tender.

5 Meanwhile, heat the oil in a frying pan and sauté the potatoes for 10–15 minutes, until cooked and golden.

6 Lift out the dried lime and discard. Spoon the meat on to a warmed, large serving dish and scatter the sautéed potatoes on top. Serve the khoresh with cooked rice.

COOK'S TIPS

Dried limes (*Limu amani*) are available in all Middle Eastern shops. However, if you have difficulty obtaining them, use the juice of either 2 limes or 1 lemon instead. If you prefer, you can use beef in place of the lamb in this khoresh.

Energy 463Kcal/1941kJ; Protein 30.3g; Carbohydrate 35.1g, of which sugars 7g; Fat 23.4g, of which saturates 10g; Cholesterol 99mg; Calcium 45mg; Fibre 3.6g; Sodium 162mg.

TURKISH SAUTÉED LAMB WITH YOGURT

MEAT IS OFTEN STEWED OR COOKED ON THE BARBECUE. THIS EXCEPTION COMES FROM TURKEY. LAMB IS MARINATED IN YOGURT, PAN-FRIED, AND LAYERED WITH COOKED TOMATOES OVER TOASTED BREAD.

SERVES FOUR

INGREDIENTS
    450g/1lb lean lamb, preferably
       boned leg, cubed
    40g/1½oz/3 tbsp butter
    4 tomatoes, skinned and chopped
    4 thick slices of white or brown
       bread, crusts removed
    250ml/8fl oz/1 cup Greek
       (US strained plain) yogurt
    2 garlic cloves, crushed
    salt and ground black pepper
    paprika and fresh mint leaves,
       to garnish
For the marinade
    120ml/4fl oz/½ cup Greek
       (US strained plain) yogurt
    1 large onion, grated

1 First make the marinade: blend together the yogurt, onion and a little seasoning in a large bowl. Add the cubed lamb, toss to coat all over, and then cover loosely with clear film (plastic wrap) and leave to marinate in a cool place for at least 1 hour.

2 Melt half the butter in a frying pan and fry the meat for 5–10 minutes, until cooked and tender, but still moist. Transfer to a plate using a slotted spoon and keep warm while cooking the tomatoes.

VARIATION
You can also use lean beef or skinless chicken breast fillets, instead of lamb, for this recipe.

3 Melt the remaining butter in the same pan and fry the tomatoes for 4–5 minutes, until soft. Meanwhile, toast the bread and arrange in the bottom of a shallow serving dish.

4 Season the tomatoes and then spread over the toasted bread in an even layer.

5 Blend the yogurt and garlic together and season with salt and pepper. Spoon evenly over the tomatoes.

6 Arrange the pan-fried lamb in a layer on top. Sprinkle with paprika and mint leaves and serve at once.

Energy 463Kcal/1939kJ; Protein 30.3g; Carbohydrate 25.2g, of which sugars 4.8g; Fat 28.3g, of which saturates 14.4g; Cholesterol 107mg; Calcium 158mg; Fibre 1.4g; Sodium 436mg.

KEBAB BAHRG

THESE KEBABS ARE SO POPULAR IN THEIR NATIVE IRAN THAT MANY RESTAURANTS SERVE NOTHING ELSE. THE MEAT IS NOT CUBED, BUT INSTEAD IS CUT INTO STRIPS BEFORE BEING MARINATED AND THREADED ON TO SKEWERS. TOMATOES ARE GRILLED ON SEPARATE SKEWERS.

SERVES FOUR

INGREDIENTS
450g/1lb lean lamb or beef fillet
2–3 saffron threads
1 large onion, grated
4–6 tomatoes, halved
15ml/1 tbsp butter, melted
salt and ground black pepper
45ml/3 tbsp sumac (see Cook's Tip),
   to garnish (optional)
cooked rice, to serve

1 Using a sharp knife remove and discard any excess fat from the meat and cut the meat into strips, 1cm/½in thick and 4cm/1½in long.

COOK'S TIP
Sumac is made from red berries that are dried and crushed to a powder.

2 Soak the saffron in 15ml/1 tbsp boiling water, pour into a small bowl and mix with the grated onion. Add to the meat and stir a few times so that the meat is thoroughly coated. Cover loosely with clear film (plastic wrap) and leave to marinate in the refrigerator overnight.

3 Season the meat with salt and pepper and then thread it on to flat skewers, aligning the strips in neat rows. Thread the tomatoes on to two separate skewers.

4 Grill the kebabs and tomatoes over hot charcoal for 10–12 minutes, basting with butter and turning occasionally. Serve with cooked rice, sprinkled with sumac, if you like.

SHISH KEBAB

ONE OF THE FIRST MIDDLE EASTERN DISHES TO ACHIEVE GLOBAL POPULARITY, SHISH KEBAB IS BELIEVED TO DATE FROM THE DAYS OF THE OTTOMAN EMPIRE, WHEN SOLDIERS GRILLED MEAT ON THEIR SWORDS OVER OPEN FIRES. THE LAMB CUBES ARE ALTERNATED WITH COLOURFUL VEGETABLES.

SERVES FOUR

INGREDIENTS
450g/1lb boned leg of lamb, cubed
1 large green (bell) pepper, seeded
   and cut into squares
1 large yellow (bell) pepper, seeded
   and cut into squares
8 baby onions, halved
225g/8oz button (white) mushrooms
4 tomatoes, halved
15ml/1 tbsp melted butter
bulgur wheat, to serve
For the marinade
45ml/3 tbsp olive oil
juice of 1 lemon
2 garlic cloves, crushed
1 large onion, grated
15ml/1 tbsp chopped fresh oregano
salt and ground black pepper

1 First make the marinade: blend together the oil, lemon juice, garlic, onion, chopped oregano and seasoning. Place the meat in a shallow, non-metallic dish and pour over the marinade.

2 Cover with clear film (plastic wrap) and leave to marinate in the refrigerator for 2–3 hours, or overnight.

3 Thread the cubes of lamb on to skewers, alternating with pieces of green and yellow pepper, onions and mushrooms. Thread the tomatoes on to separate skewers.

4 Grill the kebabs and tomatoes over hot charcoal for 10–12 minutes, basting with butter and turning occasionally. Serve with bulgur wheat.

TOP Energy 268Kcal/1119kJ; Protein 23.5g; Carbohydrate 7.9g, of which sugars 6.5g; Fat 16.1g, of which saturates 7.9g; Cholesterol 94mg; Calcium 32mg; Fibre 1.9g; Sodium 130mg.
BOTTOM Energy 340Kcal/1417kJ; Protein 25g; Carbohydrate 11.7g, of which sugars 10.3g; Fat 21.8g, of which saturates 7.3g; Cholesterol 86mg; Calcium 36mg; Fibre 3.4g; Sodium 111mg.

LEBANESE KIBBEH

LAMB PLAYS A DUAL ROLE IN THIS, LEBANON'S NATIONAL DISH. THE GROUND MEAT IS MIXED WITH
BULGUR WHEAT AND THEN WRAPPED AROUND A SECOND LAMB MIXTURE, THIS TIME WITH SPICES AND
NUTS. KIBBEH IS OFTEN MADE INTO MEATBALLS, BUT THIS TRAY VERSION IS POPULAR, TOO.

SERVES SIX

INGREDIENTS
    115g/4oz/⅔ cup bulgur wheat
    450g/1lb finely minced (ground)
        lean lamb
    1 large onion, grated
    15ml/1 tbsp melted butter
    salt and ground black pepper
    sprigs of fresh mint, to garnish
    cooked rice, to serve
For the filling
    30ml/2 tbsp oil
    1 onion, finely chopped
    225g/8oz minced (ground) lamb
        or veal
    50g/2oz/⅓ cup pine nuts
    2.5ml/½ tsp ground allspice
For the yogurt dip
    600ml/1 pint/2½ cups Greek
        (US strained plain) yogurt
    2–3 garlic cloves, crushed
    15–30ml/1–2 tbsp chopped
        fresh mint

1 Preheat the oven to 190°C/375°F/
Gas 5. Rinse the bulgur wheat in a sieve
and squeeze out the excess moisture.

2 Mix the lamb, onion and seasoning in
a bowl, kneading the mixture to make a
thick paste. Add the bulgur wheat and
mix well. Set aside.

VARIATION
Use finely minced (ground) lean beef
instead of lamb.

3 To make the filling, heat the oil in a
frying pan and fry the onion until
golden. Add the lamb or veal and cook,
stirring, until evenly browned and then
add the pine nuts, allspice and salt
and pepper.

4 Oil a large baking dish and spread
half of the meat and bulgur wheat
mixture over the bottom. Spoon over the
filling and top with a second layer of
the remaining meat and bulgur wheat,
pressing down firmly with the back of
a spoon.

5 Pour the melted butter over the
top and then bake in the oven for
40–45 minutes, until browned on top.

6 Meanwhile make the yogurt dip: blend
together the yogurt and garlic, spoon
into a serving bowl and sprinkle with the
chopped mint.

7 Cut the cooked kibbeh into squares or
rectangles and serve garnished with
mint sprigs and accompanied by
cooked rice and the yogurt dip.

Energy 452Kcal/1883kJ; Protein 29.7g; Carbohydrate 22.8g, of which sugars 11.5g; Fat 27.7g, of which saturates 9.7g; Cholesterol 93mg; Calcium 230mg; Fibre 1.1g; Sodium 178mg.

SHISH BARAK

THIS LEBANESE SPECIALITY IS A FAVOURITE LUNCHTIME DISH IN THE RESTAURANTS OF BEIRUT.
DUMPLINGS FILLED WITH LAMB, ONION AND NUTS ARE SIMMERED IN A YOGURT AND EGG SAUCE.

SERVES FOUR

INGREDIENTS
    30ml/2 tbsp olive oil
    1 large onion, chopped
    60ml/4 tbsp pine nuts or
      chopped walnuts
    450g/1lb minced (ground) lamb
    25g/1oz/2 tbsp butter
    3 garlic cloves, crushed
    15ml/1 tbsp chopped fresh mint
    salt and ground black pepper
    fresh mint leaves, to garnish
    cooked rice and green salad, to serve
For the dough
    5ml/1 tsp salt
    225g/8oz/2 cups plain
      (all-purpose) flour
For the yogurt sauce
    2 litres/3½ pints/8 cups natural
      (plain) yogurt
    1 egg, beaten
    15ml/1 tbsp cornflour (cornstarch),
      blended with 15ml/1 tbsp
      cold water
    salt and white pepper

1 First make the dough: mix the salt and the flour together and then stir in enough water for the dough to hold together. Cover and leave to rest for 1 hour.

2 Heat the oil in a large frying pan and fry the onion for 3–4 minutes, until soft. Add the pine nuts or walnuts and fry until golden. Stir in the meat and cook until brown. Season, then remove the pan from the heat.

3 Roll out the dough thinly on a floured board. Cut into small rounds 5–6cm/ 2–2½in in diameter. Place 5ml/1 tsp of filling on each one, fold the pastry over and firmly press the edges together to seal. Bring the ends together to form a handle.

4 Meanwhile, make the yogurt sauce: pour the yogurt into a pan and beat in the egg and cornflour mixture. Season with salt and white pepper and slowly bring to the boil, stirring constantly.

5 Cook over a gentle heat until the sauce thickens and then carefully drop in the dumplings and simmer for about 20 minutes.

6 Spoon the dumplings and sauce on to warmed serving plates. Melt the butter in a small frying pan and fry the garlic until golden. Stir in the chopped mint, cook briefly and then pour over the dumplings. Garnish with mint leaves and serve with rice and a green salad.

Energy 820Kcal/3441kJ; Protein 55.4g; Carbohydrate 86.1g, of which sugars 41.8g; Fat 31.5g, of which saturates 13g; Cholesterol 153mg; Calcium 1061mg; Fibre 2.6g; Sodium 1062mg.

LAMB AND VEGETABLE PILAU

ALTHOUGH MANY PEOPLE ASSOCIATE THE PILAU WITH INDIA, THIS METHOD OF COOKING RICE HAS A CLOSE ASSOCIATION WITH THE MIDDLE EAST. ANCIENT PERSIANS CALLED THE DISH PULAW, AND INVENTED EXCITING VARIATIONS, INTRODUCING FRUIT AS WELL AS VEGETABLES AND SPICES.

SERVES FOUR

INGREDIENTS
For the meat curry
- 450g/1lb boned shoulder of lamb, cubed
- 2.5ml/½ tsp dried thyme
- 2.5ml/½ tsp paprika
- 5ml/1 tsp garam masala
- 1 garlic clove, crushed
- 25ml/1½ tbsp vegetable oil
- 900ml/1½ pints/3¾ cups lamb stock or water
- salt and ground black pepper

For the rice
- 30ml/2 tbsp butter or margarine
- 1 onion, chopped
- 175g/6oz potato, diced
- 1 carrot, sliced
- ½ red (bell) pepper, seeded and chopped
- 115g/4oz green cabbage, sliced
- 1 fresh green chilli, seeded and finely chopped
- 60ml/4 tbsp natural (plain) yogurt
- 2.5ml/½ tsp ground cumin
- 5 green cardamom pods
- 2 garlic cloves, crushed
- 350g/12oz/1¾ cups basmati rice
- about 50g/2oz/⅓ cup cashew nuts

1 To make the curry, place the lamb in a large bowl and add the thyme, paprika, garam masala, garlic and salt and pepper. Mix, then cover and set aside to marinate for 2–3 hours.

2 Heat the oil in a large pan and fry the lamb, in batches if necessary, over a medium heat for 5–6 minutes, until browned.

3 Add the stock or water, stir well and then cook, covered, for 35–40 minutes, until the lamb is just tender. Transfer the lamb to a plate or bowl and pour the liquid into a measuring jug (cup), topping up with water if necessary, to make 600ml/1 pint/2½ cups. Set aside.

4 To make the rice, melt the butter or margarine and fry the onion, potato and carrot for 5 minutes.

5 Add the red pepper, cabbage, chilli, yogurt, spices, garlic and the reserved meat stock. Stir well, cover, and then simmer gently for 5–10 minutes, until the cabbage has wilted.

6 Stir in the rice and lamb, cover and simmer over a low heat for 20 minutes, until the rice is cooked. Sprinkle in the cashew nuts and season to taste with salt and pepper. Serve hot.

VARIATIONS
If you prefer, fewer vegetables can be used for this dish and cubed chicken or minced lamb substituted for the cubed lamb. Basmati rice is ideal, but long grain rice may be used instead. The amount of liquid can be varied, depending on whether firm, or well-cooked rice is preferred.

Energy 751Kcal/3135kJ; Protein 33.7g; Carbohydrate 86.3g, of which sugars 7.3g; Fat 30.1g, of which saturates 11.6g; Cholesterol 102mg; Calcium 88mg; Fibre 2.3g; Sodium 200mg.

TAGINE OF BEEF WITH PEAS AND SAFFRON

EVER SINCE THE PERSIANS DISCOVERED THAT THE BRILLIANT ORANGE STIGMAS OF A TINY WILD FLOWER COULD BE USED TO COLOUR AND FLAVOUR FOOD, SAFFRON HAS BEEN HIGHLY PRIZED, NOT ONLY IN THE MIDDLE EAST, BUT ALSO IN MEDITERRANEAN COUNTRIES. THE SPICE IS CULTIVATED COMMERCIALLY IN MOROCCO AND IS A FAVOURITE INGREDIENT IN DISHES LIKE THIS CLASSIC FRESH PEA AND PRESERVED LEMON TAGINE.

SERVES SIX

INGREDIENTS

 1.2kg/2½lb chuck steak or stewing
   beef, trimmed and cubed
 30ml/2 tbsp olive oil
 1 onion, chopped
 25g/1oz fresh root ginger, peeled and
   finely chopped
 5ml/1 tsp ground ginger
 pinch of cayenne pepper
 pinch of saffron threads
 1.2kg/2½lb shelled fresh peas
 2 tomatoes, skinned and chopped
 1 preserved lemon, chopped
 a handful of brown kalamata olives
 salt and ground black pepper
 bread or couscous, to serve

1 Put the cubed meat in a tagine, flameproof casserole or heavy pan with the olive oil, onion, fresh and ground ginger, cayenne and saffron and season with salt and pepper. Pour in enough water to cover the meat completely and then bring to the boil. Reduce the heat and then cover and simmer for about 1½ hours, until the meat is very tender. Cook for a little longer, if necessary.

2 Add the peas, tomatoes, preserved lemon and olives. Stir well and cook, uncovered, for about 10 minutes, or until the peas are tender and the sauce has reduced. Check the seasoning and serve with bread or plain couscous.

Energy 492Kcal/2049kJ; Protein 57.9g; Carbohydrate 25.6g, of which sugars 7g; Fat 18.2g, of which saturates 6g; Cholesterol 126mg; Calcium 61mg; Fibre 10.1g; Sodium 134mg.

SPICY BEEF KOFTAS <u>WITH</u> CHICKPEA PURÉE

WHEREVER YOU GO IN THE MIDDLE EAST YOU WILL ENCOUNTER THESE TASTY KEBABS, AS STREET FOOD, ON BARBECUES, AT BEACH BARS AND AT FAMILY MEALS. THE TASK OF POUNDING THE MEAT — TRADITIONALLY PERFORMED BY HAND USING A MORTAR AND PESTLE — IS MUCH EASIER IN A FOOD PROCESSOR. IT TAKES JUST A FEW MINUTES TO MOULD THE MIXTURE AROUND THE SKEWERS, AND THEY DON'T TAKE LONG TO COOK. CHICKPEA PURÉE IS THE TRADITIONAL ACCOMPANIMENT.

SERVES SIX

INGREDIENTS

500g/1¼lb finely minced
  (ground) beef
1 onion, grated
10ml/2 tsp ground cumin
10ml/2 tsp ground coriander
10ml/2 tsp paprika
4ml/¾ tsp cayenne pepper
5ml/1 tsp salt
small bunch of fresh flat leaf parsley,
  finely chopped
small bunch of fresh coriander
  (cilantro), finely chopped
For the chickpea purée
225g/8oz/1¼ cups dried chickpeas,
  soaked overnight, drained
  and cooked
50ml/2fl oz/¼ cup olive oil
juice of 1 lemon
2 garlic cloves, crushed
5ml/1 tsp cumin seeds
30ml/2 tbsp light tahini paste
60ml/4 tbsp thick Greek (US strained
  plain) yogurt
40g/1½oz/3 tbsp butter, melted
salt and ground black pepper
salad and bread, to serve

1 Mix the minced beef with the onion, cumin, ground coriander, paprika, cayenne, salt, chopped parsley and fresh coriander. Knead the mixture well, then pound it until smooth in a mortar with a pestle or in a blender or food processor. Place in a dish, cover and leave to stand in a cool place for 1 hour.

2 Meanwhile, make the chickpea purée. Preheat the oven to 200ºC/400ºF/Gas 6. In a blender or food processor, process the chickpeas with the olive oil, lemon juice, garlic, cumin seeds, tahini and yogurt until well mixed. Season with salt and pepper, tip the purée into an ovenproof dish, cover with foil and heat through in the oven for 20 minutes.

3 Divide the meat mixture into six portions and mould each on to a metal skewer, so that the meat resembles a fat sausage. Preheat the grill (broiler) on the hottest setting and cook the kebabs for 4–5 minutes on each side.

4 Melt the butter and pour it over the hot chickpea purée. Serve the kebabs with the hot chickpea purée. Serve with salad and bread.

Energy 456Kcal/1898kJ; Protein 26.6g; Carbohydrate 21.8g, of which sugars 3.5g; Fat 29.8g, of which saturates 10.7g; Cholesterol 64mg; Calcium 153mg; Fibre 5.4g; Sodium 463mg.

COUSCOUS WITH LAMB CUTLETS AND FENNEL

THIS STYLE OF COUSCOUS DISH IS OFTEN SERVED WITH SOUR PICKLES, SUCH AS CABBAGE AND HOT PEPPERS. BUTCHERS IN THE MIDDLE EAST PREPARE THIN LAMB CUTLETS, SOMETIMES DESCRIBED AS RIB CHOPS, FOR GRILLING OR FRYING. ASK YOUR BUTCHER TO DO THE SAME FOR YOU.

SERVES FOUR

INGREDIENTS
45ml/3 tbsp olive oil
2 onions, quartered
4 garlic cloves, chopped
30–45ml/2–3 tbsp tomato
    purée (paste)
10ml/2 tsp harissa
4 fennel bulbs, stalks removed
    and quartered (feathery fronds
    reserved)
50g/2oz/¼ cup butter
8 thin lamb cutlets (US
    rib chops)
salt and ground black pepper

For the couscous
2.5ml/½ tsp salt
400ml/14fl oz/1⅔ cups warm water
350g/12oz/2 cups medium couscous
30ml/2 tbsp sunflower oil
knob (pat) of butter, diced

1 Heat the olive oil in a heavy pan, add the onions and garlic and cook for 15 minutes, until softened. Mix the tomato purée with the harissa and dilute with a little water. Pour it into the pan with 600ml/1 pint/2½ cups water. Bring to the boil and add the fennel. Reduce the heat, cover and cook for about 10 minutes, until tender.

2 Meanwhile, prepare the couscous. Stir the salt into the warm water. Place the couscous in a bowl and cover with the water, stirring. Set aside for 10 minutes. Using your fingers, rub the sunflower oil into the couscous. Set aside.

3 Use a slotted spoon to lift the vegetables from the cooking liquid and transfer to a covered dish; keep warm. Boil the liquid to reduce it. Melt the butter in a heavy frying pan, add the lamb cutlets and brown on both sides. Add the cutlets to the reduced liquid and simmer for 15 minutes, until tender.

4 Preheat the oven to 180°C/350°F/ Gas 4. Turn the couscous into an ovenproof dish and arrange the diced butter on top. Chop the fennel fronds and sprinkle over the couscous. Cover with foil and bake in the oven for about 20 minutes.

5 Put the vegetables in the pan with the lamb and heat through. Fluff up the couscous then mound it on to a serving dish. Place the cutlets around the edge and spoon the vegetables over. Moisten with the cooking liquid and serve.

COOK'S TIP
Crunchy pickles make a delicious accompaniment to serve with this dish and are easy to make. Simply combine whole or chopped raw vegetables with white wine vinegar mixed with a little salt and leave to soak for about 3 weeks.

Energy 688Kcal/2862kJ; Protein 35.6g; Carbohydrate 54.5g, of which sugars 7.7g; Fat 37.7g, of which saturates 14.3g; Cholesterol 137mg; Calcium 95mg; Fibre 5.9g; Sodium 421mg.

TAGINE OF SPICED KEFTA WITH LEMON

THIS NORTH AFRICAN DISH KNOWS NO BOUNDARIES. IT CAN BE FOUND IN THE TINIEST RURAL VILLAGES, IN STREET STALLS IN THE TOWNS AND CITIES, AND IN THE FINEST RESTAURANTS OF CASABLANCA, FEZ AND MARRAKESH. KEFTA ARE LAMB MEATBALLS, FLAVOURED WITH ONION, HERBS AND SPICES. POACHED IN A BUTTERY GINGER AND LEMON SAUCE, WITH PLENTY OF CORIANDER, THEY TASTE WONDERFUL. BREAD FOR MOPPING UP THE JUICES IS ESSENTIAL.

SERVES FOUR

INGREDIENTS
    450g/1lb finely minced
      (ground) lamb
    3 large onions, grated
    small bunch of fresh flat leaf
      parsley, chopped
    5–10ml/1–2 tsp ground cinnamon
    5ml/1 tsp ground cumin
    pinch of cayenne pepper
    40g/1½oz/3 tbsp butter
    25g/1oz fresh root ginger, peeled
      and finely chopped
    1 fresh hot chilli, seeded and
      finely chopped
    pinch of saffron threads
    small bunch of fresh coriander
      (cilantro), finely chopped
    juice of 1 lemon
    300ml/½ pint/1¼ cups water
    1 lemon, quartered
    salt and ground black pepper

1 To make the kefta, pound the minced lamb in a bowl by using your hand to lift it up and slap it back down into the bowl. Knead in half the grated onions, the parsley, cinnamon, cumin and cayenne pepper. Season with salt and pepper, and continue pounding the mixture by hand for a few minutes. Break off pieces of the mixture and shape them into walnut-size balls.

2 In a lidded heavy frying pan, melt the butter and add the remaining onions with the ginger, chilli and saffron. Cook until the onions just begin to colour, stirring frequently, then stir in the chopped coriander and lemon juice.

3 Pour in the water, season with salt and bring to the boil. Drop in the kefta, reduce the heat and cover the pan. Poach the kefta gently, turning them occasionally, for about 20 minutes.

4 Remove the lid, tuck the lemon quarters around the kefta, raise the heat a little and cook, uncovered, for a further 10 minutes to reduce the liquid slightly.

5 Garnish with parsley and serve the kefka hot, straight from the pan with lots of fresh crusty bread to mop up the delicious juices.

Energy 362Kcal/1503kJ; Protein 24.5g; Carbohydrate 12.9g, of which sugars 9.3g; Fat 24g, of which saturates 12.2g; Cholesterol 108mg; Calcium 134mg; Fibre 4g; Sodium 155mg.

CHICKEN
AND POULTRY

In the Middle East, chicken is second only to lamb

in popularity. This chapter shows the different

approaches adopted by Middle Eastern cooks. From

Iran we discover Khoresh, a soup-like stew served over

rice, together with a delicious chicken yogurt dish,

while Lebanese Chicken Kebabs are well worth

making a fuss about.

CHICKEN KDRA WITH CHICKPEAS AND ALMONDS

A KDRA IS A TYPE OF TAGINE THAT IS TRADITIONALLY COOKED WITH SMEN, A STRONGLY FLAVOURED CLARIFIED BUTTER, AND PLENTY OF ONIONS. THE ALMONDS IN THIS RECIPE ARE PRE-COOKED UNTIL SOFT, ADDING AN INTERESTING TEXTURE AND FLAVOUR TO THE LIGHTLY SPICED CHICKEN.

SERVES FOUR

INGREDIENTS

75g/3oz/½ cup blanched almonds
75g/3oz/½ cup chickpeas,
  soaked overnight and drained
4 part-boned chicken breast
  portions, skinned
50g/2oz/¼ cup butter
2.5ml/½ tsp saffron threads
2 Spanish onions, thinly sliced
900ml/1½ pints/3¾ cups
  chicken stock
1 small cinnamon stick
60ml/4 tbsp chopped fresh flat leaf
  parsley, plus extra to garnish
lemon juice, to taste
salt and ground black pepper

1 Place the almonds in a pan of water and simmer for 1½–2 hours until fairly soft, then drain and set aside.

2 Cook the chickpeas in a pan of boiling water for 1–1½ hours until they are completely soft. Drain the chickpeas, then place in a bowl of cold water and rub with your fingers to remove the skins. Discard the skins and drain.

3 Place the chicken portions in a pan, together with the butter, half of the saffron, salt and plenty of black pepper. Heat gently, stirring, until the butter has melted.

4 Add the onions and stock, bring to the boil and then add the chickpeas and cinnamon stick. Cover and cook very gently for 45–60 minutes.

5 Transfer the chicken to a serving plate and keep warm. Bring the sauce to the boil and simmer until reduced, stirring frequently. Add the almonds, parsley and remaining saffron and cook for 2–3 minutes. Sharpen the sauce with a little lemon juice, then pour over the chicken and serve, garnished with extra parsley.

CHICKEN WITH TOMATOES AND HONEY

COOKING THE TOMATOES VERY SLOWLY WITH THE AROMATIC SPICES GIVES THE SAUCE FOR THIS CHICKEN DISH A WONDERFULLY INTENSE FLAVOUR, WHICH MELLOWS WHEN THE HONEY IS STIRRED IN.

SERVES FOUR

INGREDIENTS

30ml/2 tbsp sunflower oil
25g/1oz/2 tbsp butter
4 chicken quarters or 1 whole
  chicken, quartered
1 onion, grated or very
  finely chopped
1 garlic clove, crushed
5ml/1 tsp ground cinnamon
good pinch of ground ginger
1.3–1.6kg/3–3½lb tomatoes,
  skinned, cored and roughly chopped
30ml/2 tbsp clear honey
50g/2oz/⅓ cup blanched almonds
15ml/1 tbsp sesame seeds
salt and ground black pepper
Moroccan corn bread, to serve

1 Heat the oil and butter in a large, flameproof casserole. Add the chicken quarters and cook over a medium heat for about 3 minutes, until browned.

2 Add the onion, garlic, cinnamon, ginger, tomatoes and seasoning, and heat gently until the tomatoes begin to bubble.

3 Lower the heat, cover and simmer very gently for 1 hour, stirring and turning the chicken occasionally, until it is completely cooked through.

4 Transfer the chicken pieces to a plate and then increase the heat and cook the tomatoes until the sauce is reduced to a thick purée, stirring frequently. Stir in the honey, cook for 1 minute and then return the chicken to the pan and cook for 2–3 minutes to heat through. Dry-fry the almonds and sesame seeds or toast under the grill (broiler).

5 Transfer the chicken and sauce to a warmed serving dish and sprinkle with the almonds and sesame seeds. Serve with Moroccan corn bread.

TOP Energy 477Kcal/1994kJ; Protein 46g; Carbohydrate 21g, of which sugars 8.7g; Fat 23.9g, of which saturates 7.9g; Cholesterol 132mg; Calcium 146mg; Fibre 5.9g; Sodium 185mg.
BOTTOM Energy 610Kcal/2539kJ; Protein 37.7g; Carbohydrate 16.8g, of which sugars 16.4g; Fat 44g, of which saturates 11.4g; Cholesterol 206mg; Calcium 92mg; Fibre 4.5g; Sodium 211mg.

PALAVER CHICKEN

IT IS SAID THAT THIS STEW GAINED ITS INTRIGUING NAME BECAUSE OF THE ARGUMENTS THAT SURROUNDED THE RIGHT WAY TO COOK IT. PALAVER CAN BE MADE WITH BEEF, CHICKEN OR FISH AND ALWAYS INCLUDES A GREEN VEGETABLE SUCH AS BITTERLEAF. SPINACH IS SUBSTITUTED HERE.

SERVES FOUR

INGREDIENTS
  675g/1½lb skinless, boneless
    chicken breast fillets
  2 garlic cloves, crushed
  30ml/2 tbsp butter or margarine
  30ml/2 tbsp palm or vegetable oil
  1 onion, finely chopped
  4 tomatoes, skinned and chopped
  30ml/2 tbsp peanut butter
  600ml/1 pint/2½ cups chicken stock
    or water
  1 fresh thyme sprig or 5ml/1 tsp
    dried thyme
  225g/8oz frozen leaf spinach,
    defrosted and chopped
  1 fresh red or green chilli, seeded
    and chopped
  salt and ground black pepper

1 Cut the chicken breast fillets into thin slices, place in a bowl and stir in the garlic and a little salt and pepper.

2 Melt the butter or margarine in a large frying pan and fry the chicken over a medium heat, turning once or twice to brown evenly. Transfer to a plate using a slotted spoon and set aside.

3 Heat the oil in a large pan and fry the onion and tomatoes over a high heat for 5 minutes, until soft.

4 Reduce the heat, add the peanut butter and half of the stock or water and blend together well.

5 Cook for 4–5 minutes, stirring all the time to prevent the peanut butter burning, then add the remaining stock or water, thyme, spinach, chilli and seasoning. Stir in the chicken slices and cook over a medium heat for about 10–15 minutes, until the chicken is cooked through.

6 Pour the chicken mixture into a warmed serving dish and serve with boiled yams, rice or ground rice.

COOK'S TIPS
If you're short of time, frozen spinach is more convenient, but chopped fresh spinach, adds a fresher flavour to this recipe. Egusi – ground melon seed – can be used instead of peanut butter.

Energy 387Kcal/1615kJ; Protein 41.1g; Carbohydrate 7.2g, of which sugars 5.8g; Fat 21.7g, of which saturates 7.3g; Cholesterol 89mg; Calcium 131mg; Fibre 2.9g; Sodium 280mg.

KHORESH FESENJAN

A KHORESH IS A THICK STEW-LIKE SAUCE WHICH IS SERVED OVER RICE IN IRAN. THIS FAMOUS VERSION OWES ITS SUPERB FLAVOUR TO POMEGRANATES AND WALNUTS. KHORESH FESENJAN IS OFTEN SERVED ON FESTIVE OCCASIONS, WHEN WILD DUCK IS USED INSTEAD OF CHICKEN.

SERVES FOUR

INGREDIENTS

30ml/2 tbsp vegetable oil
4 chicken portions (leg or breast)
1 large onion, grated
250ml/8fl oz/1 cup water
115g/4oz/1 cup finely
  chopped walnuts
75ml/5 tbsp pomegranate purée
15ml/1 tbsp tomato purée (paste)
30ml/2 tbsp lemon juice
15ml/1 tbsp granulated sugar
3–4 saffron threads dissolved in
  15ml/1 tbsp boiling water
salt and ground black pepper
Persian rice and salad leaves,
  to serve

1 Heat 15ml/1 tbsp of the oil in a large pan or flameproof casserole and sauté the chicken portions until golden brown.

2 Add half of the grated onion to the chicken and fry until slightly softened, then add the water and seasoning and bring to the boil. Cover the pan, reduce the heat and simmer for 15 minutes.

3 Meanwhile, heat the remaining oil in a small pan or frying pan and fry the remaining onion for 2–3 minutes, until soft.

4 Add the chopped walnuts to the onion and fry for a further 2–3 minutes over a low heat, stirring frequently and taking great care that the walnuts do not burn.

5 Stir in the pomegranate and tomato purées, lemon juice, sugar and the saffron liquid. Season to taste and then simmer over a low heat for 5 minutes.

6 Pour the walnut sauce over the chicken, ensuring all the pieces are well covered. Cover and simmer for 30–35 minutes, until the meat is cooked and the oil of the walnuts has risen to the surface.

7 Serve immediately with Persian rice and salad leaves.

COOK'S TIP
Pomegranate purée is available from Middle Eastern delicatessens.

Energy 460Kcal/1918kJ; Protein 42.1g; Carbohydrate 12.8g, of which sugars 11.2g; Fat 27g, of which saturates 2.7g; Cholesterol 105mg; Calcium 60mg; Fibre 2.5g; Sodium 148mg.

KHORESH BADEMJAN

This classic Persian dish, believed to have been a favourite of kings, is often served on festive occasions. The word bademjan means aubergines and this is a wonderful vehicle for the delicious purple vegetable. Cubes of beef can be used instead of chicken.

SERVES FOUR

INGREDIENTS
30ml/2 tbsp sunflower oil
1 whole chicken or 4 large
  chicken portions
1 large onion, chopped
2 garlic cloves, crushed
400g/14oz can chopped tomatoes
250ml/8fl oz/1 cup water
3 aubergines (eggplants), sliced
3 (bell) peppers, preferably red,
  green and yellow, seeded and sliced
30ml/2 tbsp lemon juice
15ml/1 tbsp ground cinnamon
salt and ground black pepper
Persian rice, to serve

1 Heat 15ml/1 tbsp of the oil in a large pan and fry the chicken or chicken portions on both sides for about 10 minutes until the skin is a golden brown.

2 Remove the chicken from the pan, and set aside on a warm plate. Add the chopped onion and fry for 4–5 minutes, until golden brown. Return the chicken to the pan.

3 Add the garlic, chopped tomatoes, water and seasoning to the chicken and onion. Bring to the boil, then reduce the heat and simmer slowly, covered, for 10 minutes.

4 Meanwhile, heat the remaining oil in a frying pan and fry the aubergines in batches until lightly golden. Transfer to a plate using a slotted spoon. Add the sliced peppers to the pan and fry for a few minutes, until slightly softened.

5 Place the aubergine slices over the chicken or chicken portions and then add the peppers. Sprinkle over the lemon juice and cinnamon, then cover and continue to cook over a low heat for about 45 minutes, until the chicken is cooked.

6 Transfer the chicken to a warmed serving plate and spoon the aubergines and peppers around the edge.

7 Reheat the sauce, if necessary, adjust the seasoning and pour over the chicken. Serve the khoresh with Persian rice.

VARIATION
Substitute 1 large red onion or 5–6 shallots instead of standard onion.

Energy 467Kcal/1945kJ; Protein 39.9g; Carbohydrate 18.4g, of which sugars 16.2g; Fat 26.4g, of which saturates 7.7g; Cholesterol 163mg; Calcium 63mg; Fibre 5.7g; Sodium 186mg.

TAH CHIN

IRANIANS LOVE THIS RICE DISH AND OFTEN MAKE IT WITH LAMB INSTEAD OF CHICKEN. THE NAME MEANS "ARRANGED AT THE BOTTOM OF THE POT" AND REFERS TO THE WAY THE INGREDIENTS ARE LAYERED. THE YOGURT MARINADE FLAVOURS THE CHICKEN AND MAKES IT BEAUTIFULLY TENDER.

SERVES SIX

INGREDIENTS
40g/1½oz/3 tbsp butter
1.3–1.6kg/3–3½lb chicken
1 large onion, chopped
250ml/8fl oz/1 cup chicken stock
2 eggs
475ml/16fl oz/2 cups natural
  (plain) yogurt
2–3 saffron threads, dissolved in
  15ml/1 tbsp boiling water
5ml/1 tsp ground cinnamon
450g/1lb/scant 2⅓ cups basmati
  rice, rinsed
75g/3oz zereshk (see Cook's Tip)
salt and ground black pepper
herb salad, to serve

1 Melt 25g/1oz/2 tbsp of the butter in a large pan and fry the chicken and onion for 4–5 minutes, until the onion is softened and the chicken is browned.

2 Add the chicken stock and salt and pepper, bring to the boil then reduce the heat and simmer for 45 minutes, until the stock is reduced by half.

3 Remove the pan from the heat. Remove the chicken to a plate, and when cool enough to handle, skin and bone the chicken. Cut the flesh into large pieces and place in a large bowl. Discard the bones and reserve the stock.

COOK'S TIP
Zereshk is a small sour berry that grows on trees by the waterside in the warmer part of Iran.

4 Beat the eggs and blend with the yogurt. Add the saffron liquid and ground cinnamon and season with salt and pepper. Pour over the chicken and leave to marinate for up to 2 hours.

5 Drain the rice and boil it in salted water for 5 minutes. Reduce the heat and simmer for 5 minutes until almost cooked. Drain and rinse in warm water.

6 Transfer the chicken from the yogurt mixture to a dish and mix half the rice into the yogurt.

7 Preheat the oven to 160°C/325°F/ Gas 3 and grease a large, 10cm/4in deep, ovenproof dish.

8 Place the rice and yogurt mixture in the bottom of the dish, arrange the chicken pieces in a layer on top and then add the plain rice. Sprinkle with the zereshk.

9 Mix the remaining butter with the reserved stock and pour over the rice. Cover tightly with foil and cook in the oven for 35–45 minutes.

10 Leave the dish to cool for a few minutes. Place on a cold, damp cloth which will help lift the rice from the bottom of the dish, then run a knife around the edges of the dish. Place a large flat plate over the dish and turn out. You should have a rice "cake" which can be cut into wedges. Serve hot with a herb salad.

Energy 682Kcal/2843kJ; Protein 43.4g; Carbohydrate 69g, of which sugars 8.2g; Fat 25.7g, of which saturates 10.2g; Cholesterol 220mg; Calcium 198mg; Fibre 0.6g; Sodium 250mg.

DUCK WITH WALNUTS AND POMEGRANATES

THIS IS AN EXTREMELY EXOTIC SWEET AND SOUR DISH WHICH ORIGINALLY CAME FROM PERSIA.

SERVES FOUR

INGREDIENTS
  60ml/4 tbsp olive oil
  2 onions, very thinly sliced
  2.5ml/½ tsp ground turmeric
  400g/14oz/3½ cups walnuts,
    roughly chopped
  1 litre/1¾ pints/4 cups duck or
    chicken stock
  6 pomegranates
  30ml/2 tbsp caster (superfine) sugar
  60ml/4 tbsp lemon juice
  4 duck breasts, each weighing
    about 225g/8oz
  salt and freshly ground
    black pepper

1 Heat half the oil in a frying pan, add the onions and turmeric, and cook until soft. Transfer to a saucepan, add the walnuts and stock, then season. Stir, bring to the boil and simmer, uncovered, for 20 minutes.

2 Cut the pomegranates in half and scoop out the seeds. Reserve the seeds of one pomegranate. Transfer the remaining seeds to a blender or food processor and process. Strain through a sieve, to extract the juice, and stir in the sugar and lemon juice.

3 Score the skin of the duck breasts in a lattice fashion with a knife. Heat the remaining oil in a frying pan or chargrill and place the duck breasts in it, skin side down.

4 Cook gently for 10 minutes, pouring off the fat from time to time, until the skin is dark golden and crisp. Turn them over and cook for a further 3–4 minutes. Transfer to a plate and leave to rest.

5 Deglaze the frying pan or chargrill with the pomegranate juice mixture, stirring with a wooden spoon, then add the walnut and stock mixture and simmer for about 15 minutes, or until the sauce has thickened slightly. Serve the duck breasts sliced, drizzled with a little sauce, and garnished with the reserved pomegranate seeds. Serve the remaining sauce separately.

Energy 753Kcal/3,123kJ; Protein 40.2g; Carbohydrate 13.1g, of which sugars 11.5g; Fat 62.9g, of which saturates 6.7g; Cholesterol 165mg; Calcium 105mg; Fibre 3.4g; Sodium 173mg.

CHICKEN WITH LEMONS AND OLIVES

LEMONS AND OLIVES CREATE A GENTLE FLAVOUR THAT ENHANCES ALL KINDS OF DISHES.

SERVES FOUR

INGREDIENTS
- 2.5ml/½ tsp ground cinnamon
- 2.5ml/½ tsp ground turmeric
- 1.5kg/3–3½lb chicken
- 30ml/2 tbsp olive oil
- 1 large onion, thinly sliced
- 5cm/2in fresh root ginger, grated
- 600ml/1 pint/2½ cups chicken stock
- 2 preserved lemons or limes, or fresh ones, cut into wedges
- 75g/3oz/½ cup brown olives, pitted
- 15ml/1 tbsp clear honey
- 60ml/4 tbsp chopped fresh coriander (cilantro)
- salt and freshly ground black pepper
- fresh coriander sprigs, to garnish

1 Preheat the oven to 190°C/375°F/Gas 5. Mix the ground cinnamon and turmeric in a bowl with a little salt and pepper and rub it all over the chicken skin to give an even coating.

2 Heat the oil in a large sauté or frying pan and fry the chicken on all sides until it turns golden. Transfer the chicken to an ovenproof dish.

3 Add the sliced onion to the pan and fry for 3 minutes. Stir in the grated ginger and the chicken stock and bring it just to the boil.

4 Pour the chicken stock mixture over the chicken, cover with a lid and bake in the oven for 30 minutes.

5 Remove the chicken from the oven and add the lemons or limes, brown olives and honey.

6 Bake the dish, uncovered, for a further 45 minutes until the chicken is tender. Stir in the fresh coriander and season to taste. Garnish with coriander sprigs and serve at once.

Energy 604kcal/2503kJ; Protein 46.5g; Carbohydrate 4.5g, of which sugars 4.1g; Fat 44.3g, of which saturates 12.2g; Cholesterol 240mg; Calcium 59mg; Fibre 1.4g; Sodium 647mg.

LEBANESE CHICKEN KEBABS

CHICKEN KEBABS ARE PREPARED IN MUCH THE SAME WAY ALL OVER THE MIDDLE EAST AND ARE A GREAT FAVOURITE EVERYWHERE. KEEP THE CHICKEN PIECES QUITE LARGE, SO THEY STAY MOIST.

SERVES SIX TO EIGHT

INGREDIENTS
    2 small chickens
    1 large onion, grated
    2 garlic cloves, crushed
    120ml/4fl oz/½ cup olive oil
    juice of 1 lemon
    5ml/1 tsp paprika
    2–3 saffron threads, dissolved in
        15ml/1 tbsp boiling water
    salt and ground black pepper
    naan bread or pitta bread, to serve

1 Cut the chickens into small pieces, removing the bones if preferred, and place the portions in a shallow non-metallic bowl.

2 Mix the onion, garlic, olive oil, lemon juice, paprika and saffron liquid together, and season with salt and pepper.

3 Pour the marinade over the chicken, turning the chicken so that all the pieces are coated evenly.

4 Cover the bowl loosely with clear film (plastic wrap) and leave to marinate in a cool place for at least 2 hours.

5 Thread the chicken on to long, metal skewers. If barbecuing, once the coals are ready, cook for 10–15 minutes each side. Or, if you prefer, cook under a medium-hot grill (broiler) for about 10–15 minutes each side.

6 Serve with rice and salad. Or remove boneless chicken from the skewers and serve it in pitta as a sandwich, with a garlicky yogurt sauce.

BAKED POUSSINS WITH YOGURT AND SAFFRON

IN MIDDLE EASTERN MARKETS, CHICKENS ARE OFTEN ON THE SMALL SIDE, AND ARE OFTEN SPLIT AND SPATCHCOCKED BEFORE BEING COOKED OVER THE COALS. POUSSINS CAN BE TREATED IN THE SAME WAY, AND TASTE PARTICULARLY GOOD WHEN MARINATED IN YOGURT, SAFFRON AND OTHER SPICES.

SERVES FOUR

INGREDIENTS
    475ml/16fl oz/2 cups natural
        (plain) yogurt
    60ml/4 tbsp olive oil
    1 large onion, grated
    2 garlic cloves, crushed
    2.5ml/½ tsp paprika
    2–3 saffron threads, dissolved in
        15ml/1 tbsp boiling water
    juice of 1 lemon
    4 poussins, halved
    salt and ground black pepper
    cos or romaine lettuce salad,
        to serve

1 Blend together the yogurt, olive oil, onion, garlic, paprika, saffron liquid and lemon juice, and season with salt and pepper.

2 Place the poussin halves in a shallow, non-metallic dish, pour over the marinade and then cover and allow to marinate overnight in a cool place or for at least 4 hours in the refrigerator.

3 Preheat the oven to 180°C/350°F/ Gas 4. Arrange the poussins in a greased ovenproof dish and bake in the oven for 30–45 minutes, basting frequently, until cooked. Serve with a lettuce salad.

COOK'S TIP
The poussins can also be cooked on a barbecue, for an authentic and even more delicious taste.

POUSSINS WITH COURGETTE AND APRICOT STUFFING

COUSCOUS ABSORBS THE LIQUID FROM THE COURGETTES AND MAKES A SUPERB STUFFING. QUAIL AND PARTRIDGE ARE POPULAR IN THE MIDDLE EAST, AND CAN BE USED INSTEAD OF BABY POUSSINS.

SERVES FOUR

INGREDIENTS
    4 small poussins
    about 40g/1½oz/3 tbsp butter,
      at room temperature
    5–10ml/1–2 tsp ground coriander
    1 large red (bell) pepper
    1 fresh red chilli
    15ml/1 tbsp olive oil
    120ml/4fl oz/½ cup chicken stock
    30ml/2 tbsp cornflour (cornstarch)
    salt and ground black pepper
    fresh flat leaf parsley, to garnish
For the stuffing
    525ml/17fl oz/2¼ cups chicken or
      vegetable stock
    275g/10oz/generous 1½ cups
      couscous
    2 small courgettes (zucchini)
    8 ready-to-eat dried apricots
    15ml/1 tbsp chopped fresh flat
      leaf parsley
    15ml/1 tbsp chopped fresh
      coriander (cilantro)
    juice of ½ lemon

1 First make the stuffing. Bring the stock to the boil and pour it over the couscous in a large bowl. Stir once and then set aside for 10 minutes.

2 Meanwhile, top and tail the courgettes and then grate coarsely. Roughly chop the apricots and add to the courgettes. Preheat the oven to 200°C/400°F/Gas 6.

3 When the couscous has swollen, fluff it up with a fork and then spoon 90ml/ 6 tbsp into a separate bowl and add the courgettes and chopped apricots to this. Add the chopped herbs, lemon juice and seasoning and stir to make a fairly loose stuffing. Set aside the remaining couscous for serving (see Cook's Tips).

4 Spoon the stuffing loosely into the body cavities of the poussins and secure with string or cocktail sticks. Place the birds in a medium or large flameproof roasting pan so that they fit comfortably but not too closely. Rub the butter into the skins and sprinkle with ground coriander and a little salt and pepper.

COOK'S TIPS
You can reheat the couscous in two ways: either cover the bowl with clear film (plastic wrap) and microwave on High for 2–3 minutes, stirring once or twice, or place in a colander or steamer and set over a pan of simmering water. If liked, finely chopped herbs can be added to the couscous to give colour.

5 Cut the red pepper into medium-sized strips and thinly slice the chilli, discarding the seeds and core. Place in the roasting pan around the poussins and then spoon over the olive oil.

6 Roast in the oven for 20 minutes, then reduce the oven temperature to 180°C/350°F/Gas 4. Pour the stock around the poussins and baste each one with the stock and red pepper/chilli mixture. Return the pan to the oven and roast for a further 30–35 minutes, until the poussins are cooked through and the meat juices run clear, basting occasionally with the stock.

7 When the poussins are cooked, transfer to a warmed serving plate. Blend the cornflour with 45ml/3 tbsp cold water, stir into the stock and peppers in the roasting pan and heat gently, stirring all the time, until the sauce is slightly thickened. Taste, and adjust the seasoning, and then pour into a jug or pour over the poussins. Garnish with flat leaf parsley and serve at once with the reserved couscous.

Energy 593Kcal/2477kJ; Protein 28.1g; Carbohydrate 59.4g, of which sugars 10.2g; Fat 28.5g, of which saturates 10.1g; Cholesterol 137mg; Calcium 64mg; Fibre 2.5g; Sodium 156mg.

Vegetarian
Dishes and
Accompaniments

  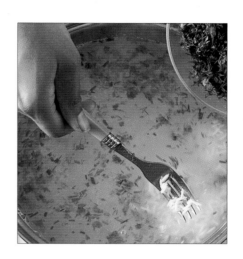

Though most main dishes in the Middle East are meat- or fish-based, or contain meat stock, there are a great variety of vegetarian appetizers, many of which can be adapted to serve as main courses. Try a tempting Chickpea and Okra Stir-fry, a Marrakesh Pizza, or Fatayer — a Turkish spinach and cheese filo pie. Bread and rice, often with flavoursome additions, are essential accompaniments to any meal.

FATAYER

This spinach and cheese filo pie is the Turkish version of that Greek favourite, spanakopita. Similar recipes are found throughout the Middle East, the Mediterranean and North Africa, the differences being in the spicing and the type of pastry used.

SERVES SIX

INGREDIENTS
    900g/2lb fresh spinach, chopped
    25g/1oz/2 tbsp butter or margarine
    2 onions, chopped
    2 garlic cloves, crushed
    275g/10oz feta cheese, crumbled
    115g/4oz/²⁄₃ cup pine nuts
    5 eggs, beaten
    2 saffron threads, dissolved in 30ml/
      2 tbsp boiling water
    5ml/1 tsp paprika
    1.5ml/¼ tsp ground cumin
    1.5ml/¼ tsp ground cinnamon
    14 sheets of filo pastry
    about 60ml/4 tbsp olive oil
    salt and ground black pepper
    lettuce leaves, to serve

1 Place the spinach in a large colander, sprinkle with a little salt, rub it into the leaves and leave for 30 minutes to drain the excess liquid.

2 Preheat the oven to 180°C/350°F/ Gas 4. Melt the butter or margarine in a large pan and fry the onions, until golden. Stir in the garlic, feta cheese and pine nuts.

3 Remove the pan from the heat and stir in the eggs, spinach, saffron water and spices. Season with salt and pepper and mix well.

VARIATION
Grated Cheddar, fresh Parmesan or any hard cheese can be used in this dish instead of the feta.

4 Grease a large rectangular baking dish. Take seven of the sheets of filo pastry and brush one side of each with a little olive oil. Place on the bottom of the dish, overlapping the sides.

5 Spoon all of the spinach mixture over the pastry and carefully drizzle 30ml/ 2 tbsp of the remaining olive oil over the top.

6 Fold the overlapping pastry over the filling. Cut the remaining pastry sheets to the dish size and brush each one with more olive oil. Arrange on top of the filling.

7 Brush with water to prevent curling and then bake in the oven for about 30 minutes, until the pastry is golden brown. Serve with the lettuce leaves.

Energy 565Kcal/2349kJ; Protein 22.7g; Carbohydrate 31.8g, of which sugars 5.6g; Fat 39.5g, of which saturates 11.9g; Cholesterol 200mg; Calcium 500mg; Fibre 4.9g; Sodium 956mg.

KUKU SABZI

THE TRADITIONAL WAY OF CELEBRATING THE NEW YEAR IN IRAN IS TO INVITE SOME FRIENDS OVER TO SHARE IN THIS BAKED EGG AND HERB DISH. IT RESEMBLES A LARGE OVEN-BAKED OMELETTE AND IS FILLED WITH FRESH VEGETABLES. CHOPPED LETTUCE IS OFTEN INCLUDED, AS ARE SPINACH AND HERBS.

SERVES FOUR TO SIX

INGREDIENTS
    2–3 saffron threads
    8 eggs
    2 leeks, trimmed and washed
    115g/4oz fresh spinach
    ½ iceberg lettuce
    4 spring onions (scallions)
    45ml/3 tbsp chopped fresh parsley
    45ml/3 tbsp chopped fresh chives
    45ml/3 tbsp chopped fresh
      coriander (cilantro)
    1 garlic clove, crushed
    30ml/2 tbsp chopped walnuts
      (optional)
    25g/1oz/2 tbsp butter
    salt and ground black pepper
    natural (plain) yogurt and pitta bread,
      to serve

1 Preheat the oven to 180°C/350°F/ Gas 4. Soak the saffron threads in 15ml/1 tbsp boiling water in a bowl.

2 Beat the eggs in a large bowl. Finely chop the leeks, spinach, lettuce and spring onions.

3 Add the chopped greens to the eggs together with the herbs, garlic, and walnuts, if using. Season with salt and pepper, add the saffron water and stir thoroughly to mix. Melt the butter in a large flameproof, ovenproof dish and pour in the vegetable and egg mixture.

4 Bake in the oven for 35–40 minutes, until the egg mixture is set and the top is golden. Serve warm or cold, cut into wedges, with yogurt and bread.

Energy 230Kcal/955kJ; Protein 15.5g; Carbohydrate 4.2g, of which sugars 3.4g; Fat 17.2g, of which saturates 6.5g; Cholesterol 394mg; Calcium 162mg; Fibre 3.5g; Sodium 225mg.

CHICKPEA AND OKRA STIR-FRY

THIS MODERN TREATMENT OF MIDDLE EASTERN INGREDIENTS TYPIFIES WHAT YOUNG PROFESSIONALS PREPARE WHEN TIME IS SHORT. THEIR MOTHERS WOULD HAVE COOKED THE CHICKPEAS THEMSELVES.

SERVES FOUR

INGREDIENTS
450g/1lb okra
15ml/1 tbsp vegetable oil
15ml/1 tbsp mustard oil
15g/½oz/1 tbsp butter
1 onion, finely chopped
1 garlic clove, crushed
2 tomatoes, finely chopped
1 fresh green chilli, seeded and
  finely chopped
2 slices of fresh root ginger, peeled
5ml/1 tsp ground cumin
15ml/1 tbsp chopped fresh
  coriander (cilantro)
400g/14oz can chickpeas, rinsed
  and drained
salt and ground black pepper

VARIATION
Use other canned beans such as black-eyed beans (peas) instead of chickpeas.

1 Wash and dry the okra, trim the ends and roughly chop the flesh.

2 Heat the vegetable and mustard oils and the butter in a large frying pan.

3 Fry the onion and garlic for 5 minutes, until the onion is slightly softened. Add the chopped tomatoes, chilli and ginger, stir well, then add the okra, cumin and chopped coriander. Simmer for 5 minutes, stirring frequently, and then stir in the chickpeas and seasoning.

4 Cook gently for a few minutes until the chickpeas are heated through, then spoon the mixture into a serving bowl and serve at once.

Energy 241Kcal/1010kJ; Protein 10.9g; Carbohydrate 22.2g, of which sugars 5.6g; Fat 12.8g, of which saturates 3.3g; Cholesterol 8mg; Calcium 231mg; Fibre 9.3g; Sodium 257mg.

IMAM BAYILDI

THE NAME OF THIS MUCH LOVED TURKISH DISH TRANSLATES AS "THE IMAM FAINTED", AND IS SAID TO REPRESENT HIS REACTION ON TASTING THE SUPERB STUFFED AUBERGINES.

SERVES SIX

INGREDIENTS

   6 aubergines (eggplants)
   120ml/8 tbsp olive oil
   2 large onions, chopped
   2 small red (bell) peppers, seeded
     and diced
   2 small green (bell) peppers, seeded
     and diced
   6 garlic cloves, crushed
   10–12 tomatoes, skinned and chopped
   60ml/4 tbsp chopped fresh parsley
   about 500ml/16fl oz/2 cup
     boiling water
   30ml/2 tbsp lemon juice
   salt and ground black pepper
   chopped fresh parsley, to garnish
   bread, salad and yogurt dip, to serve

1 Preheat the oven to 190°C/375°F/ Gas 5. Cut the aubergines in half lengthways and scoop out the flesh, reserving the shells. Set aside.

2 Heat 30ml/2 tbsp of the olive oil and fry the onion and peppers for 5–6 minutes, until both are slightly softened but not too tender.

3 Add the garlic and continue to cook for a further 2 minutes, then stir in the tomatoes, chopped parsley and aubergine flesh. Season and then stir well and fry over a medium heat for 2–3 minutes.

4 Heat the remaining oil in a separate pan and fry the aubergine shells, two at a time, on both sides.

COOK'S TIP
This flavourful dish can be made in advance and is ideal for a entertaining.

5 Stuff the shells with the sautéed vegetables. Arrange the aubergines closely together in an ovenproof dish and pour enough boiling water around the aubergines to come halfway up their sides.

6 Cover with foil and bake in the oven for 45–60 minutes, until the aubergines are tender and most of the liquid has been absorbed.

7 Place two halves of aubergine on each plate and sprinkle with a little lemon juice. Serve hot or cold, garnished with parsley and accompanied by bread, salad and a yogurt dip.

Energy 256Kcal/1064kJ; Protein 5.2g; Carbohydrate 22.8g, of which sugars 20.2g; Fat 16.6g, of which saturates 2.6g; Cholesterol 0mg; Calcium 80mg; Fibre 9g; Sodium 28mg.

BULGUR AND PINE NUT PILAFF

A VARIATION ON RICE PILAFF, THIS IS PARTICULARLY POPULAR IN SYRIA, JORDAN AND TURKEY. THE PINE NUTS ACCENTUATE THE NUTTY FLAVOUR OF THE BULGUR WHEAT.

SERVES FOUR

INGREDIENTS
   30ml/2 tbsp olive oil
   1 onion, chopped
   1 garlic clove, crushed
   5ml/1 tsp ground saffron or turmeric
   2.5ml/½ tsp ground cinnamon
   1 fresh green chilli, seeded and
      finely chopped
   600ml/1 pint/2½ cups
      vegetable stock
   150ml/¼ pint/⅔ cup white wine
   225g/8oz/1⅓ cups bulgur wheat
   15g/½oz/1 tbsp butter or margarine
   30–45ml/2–3 tbsp pine nuts
   30ml/2 tbsp chopped fresh parsley

1 Heat the oil in a pan and fry the onion until soft. Add the garlic, saffron or turmeric, ground cinnamon and chopped chilli, and fry for a few seconds more.

2 Add the stock and wine, bring to the boil, then reduce the heat and simmer for 8 minutes.

3 Rinse the bulgur wheat under cold running water, drain and add to the stock mixture. Cover and simmer gently for about 15 minutes until the stock is absorbed.

4 Melt the butter or margarine in a separate small pan, add the pine nuts and fry for a few minutes, until golden. Add to the bulgur wheat with the chopped parsley and fork through.

5 Spoon into a warmed serving dish and serve with a vegetable stew.

VARIATION
You can replace the wine with water or stock, if you prefer.

Energy 392Kcal/1637kJ; Protein 7.8g; Carbohydrate 75.7g, of which sugars 4.5g; Fat 6.1g, of which saturates 0.7g; Cholesterol 0mg; Calcium 36mg; Fibre 1.1g; Sodium 20mg.

ZERESHK POLO

THE ZERESHK, OR BARBERRIES, THAT FLAVOUR THIS DISH ARE VERY SMALL DRIED BERRIES THAT ARE
DELICIOUS WITH RICE. THEY ARE AVAILABLE FROM MOST PERSIAN AND MIDDLE EASTERN FOOD STORES.

SERVES FOUR

INGREDIENTS
    50g/2oz zereshk
    45ml/3 tbsp melted butter
    50g/2oz/⅓ cup raisins
    30ml/2 tbsp sugar
    5ml/1 tsp ground cinnamon
    5ml/1 tsp ground cumin
    350g/12oz/1¾ cups basmati rice,
        soaked in salted water for
        2 hours
    2–3 saffron threads, dissolved in
        15ml/1 tbsp boiling water
    salt

1 Thoroughly wash the zereshk in cold water at least 4–5 times to rinse off any bits of grit.

2 Heat 15ml/1 tbsp of the butter in a small frying pan and stir-fry the raisins for 1–2 minutes.

3 Add the zereshk, stir-fry for a few seconds and then add the sugar, and half of the cinnamon and cumin. Cook briefly and then set aside.

4 Drain the rice and then boil it in a pan of salted water for 5 minutes, reduce the heat and simmer for 10 minutes, until almost cooked.

5 Drain and rinse the rice in lukewarm water, and wash and dry the pan. Heat half of the remaining butter in the pan, add 15ml/1 tbsp water and stir in half of the rice.

6 Sprinkle with half of the raisin and zereshk mixture and top with all but 45ml/3 tbsp of the rice. Sprinkle over the remaining raisin mixture.

7 Blend the reserved rice with the remaining cinnamon and cumin and sprinkle over the top of the rice mixture.

8 Dribble the remaining butter over and then cover the pan with a clean dishtowel and secure with a tightly fitting lid, lifting the corners of the cloth back over the lid. Steam the rice over a very low heat for about 30–40 minutes.

9 Just before serving, mix 45ml/3 tbsp of the rice with the saffron water. Spoon the rice on to a large, flat serving dish and sprinkle the saffron rice over the top to garnish.

Energy 465Kcal/1943kJ; Protein 7g; Carbohydrate 87g, of which sugars 17.2g; Fat 9.8g, of which saturates 5.9g; Cholesterol 24mg; Calcium 32mg; Fibre 0.6g; Sodium 77mg.

CHELO <u>WITH</u> TAHDIG

IN IRAN, STEAMED RICE — CHELO — IS SERVED ALMOST EVERY DAY. THE TRADITIONAL METHOD INVOLVES SOAKING THE RICE, THEN STEAMING IT VERY SLOWLY, SO IT BECOMES SOFT AND FLUFFY, AND A CRISP GOLDEN RICE CRUST OR "TAHDIQ" FORMS ON THE BOTTOM OF THE PAN.

<u>SERVES FOUR</u>

INGREDIENTS
350g/12oz/1¾ cups long grain rice
5ml/1 tsp salt
45ml/3 tbsp melted butter
2–3 saffron threads, dissolved in
15ml/1 tbsp boiling water (optional)

1 Soak the rice in lukewarm water, salted with 15ml/1 tbsp salt, for a minimum of 2 hours.

2 When the rice has soaked, and you are ready to cook, fill a non-stick pan with fresh water, add a little salt and bring to the boil.

3 Drain the rice and stir it into the boiling water. Boil for 5 minutes, then reduce the heat and simmer for about 10 minutes, until the rice is almost cooked. Drain the rice and rinse in lukewarm water. Wash and dry the pan.

4 Heat 30ml/2 tbsp of the melted butter in the pan. Make sure it does not burn. Add 15ml/1 tbsp water and stir in the rice. Cook the rice over a very low heat for 10 minutes, and then pour over the remaining butter.

5 Cover the pan with a clean dishtowel and secure with a tightly fitting lid, lift the corners of the cloth over the lid.

6 Steam the rice for 30–40 minutes. The cloth will absorb the excess steam and the bottom of the rice will turn into a crisp, golden crust called tahdiq. This is regarded by many as the best part of the rice. To serve, if you like, mix 30–45ml/2–3 tbsp of the rice with the saffron water and sprinkle over the top of the rice.

PLAIN PERSIAN RICE

THIS IS A QUICKER, EASIER METHOD OF COOKING CHELO. DON'T SKIMP ON THE SOAKING TIME, THOUGH, AS IT SOFTENS THE GRAINS AND IMPROVES THE FLAVOUR OF THE FINISHED DISH.

<u>SERVES FOUR</u>

INGREDIENTS
750ml/1¼ pints/3 cups water
5ml/1 tsp salt
350g/12oz/1¾ cups basmati rice
40g/1½oz/3 tbsp butter

1 Place the water and salt in a pan and pour in the rice. Set aside to soak for at least 30 minutes and up to 2 hours.

2 Bring the water and rice to the boil, and then reduce the heat and simmer for 10–15 minutes, until the water is absorbed.

3 Add the butter to the rice, cover the pan with a tight-fitting lid and steam over a very low heat for about 30 minutes. Serve with Khoresh, or any other vegetarian dish.

TOP Energy 398Kcal/1659kJ; Protein 6.6g; Carbohydrate 69.9g, of which sugars 0.1g; Fat 9.7g, of which saturates 5.9g; Cholesterol 24mg; Calcium 19mg; Fibre 0g; Sodium 552mg.
BOTTOM Energy 389Kcal/1620kJ; Protein 6.5g; Carbohydrate 69.9g, of which sugars 0.1g; Fat 8.7g, of which saturates 5.2g; Cholesterol 21mg; Calcium 19mg; Fibre 0g; Sodium 552mg.

SHIRIN POLO

ALSO KNOWN AS SWEET RICE, THIS COLOURFUL DISH IS TRADITIONALLY SERVED AT IRANIAN WEDDING BANQUETS. FOR A MAIN COURSE, CHICKEN MAY BE ADDED TO THE RICE MIXTURE.

SERVES EIGHT TO TEN

INGREDIENTS
  3 oranges
  90ml/6 tbsp sugar
  45ml/3 tbsp melted butter
  5–6 carrots, cut into julienne strips
  50g/2oz/½ cup mixed chopped
    pistachios, almonds and pine nuts
  675g/1½lb/3⅓ cups basmati rice,
    soaked in salted water for 2 hours
  2–3 saffron threads, dissolved in
    15ml/1 tbsp boiling water
  salt

COOK'S TIP
Take care to cook this rice over a very low heat as it can burn easily owing to the added sugar and the natural sugar in the carrots.

1 Cut the peel from the oranges in wide strips using a potato peeler, and cut the peel into thin shreds.

2 Place the strips of peel in a pan cover with water and bring to the boil. Simmer for a few minutes, and then drain and repeat this process, until you have removed the bitter flavour of the peel.

3 Place the peel back in the pan with 45ml/3 tbsp sugar and 60ml/4 tbsp water. Bring to the boil then simmer, until reduced by half. Set aside.

4 Heat 15ml/1 tbsp of the butter in a pan and fry the carrots for 2–3 minutes. Add the remaining sugar and 60ml/4 tbsp water and simmer for 10 minutes, until the liquid has almost evaporated.

5 Stir the carrots and half of the nuts into the orange peel and set aside. Drain the rice, boil it in a pan of salted water for 5 minutes, then reduce the heat and simmer very gently for 10 minutes, until almost cooked. Drain and rinse.

6 Heat 15ml/1 tbsp of the remaining butter in the pan and add 45ml/3 tbsp water. Fork a little of the rice into the pan and spoon on some of the orange mixture. Make layers until all the mixture has been used.

7 Cook gently for 10 minutes. Pour over the remaining butter and cover with a clean dishtowel. Secure the lid and steam for 30–45 minutes. Garnish with nuts, and drizzle over the saffron water.

RICE WITH FRESH HERBS

CORIANDER, CHIVES AND DILL LOOK PRETTY SCATTERED AMONG THE RICE GRAINS IN THIS POPULAR MIDDLE EASTERN ACCOMPANIMENT. SERVE IT WITH A HIGHLY SPICED MAIN COURSE.

SERVES FOUR

INGREDIENTS
  350g/12oz/1¾ cups basmati rice,
    soaked in salted water for 2 hours
  30ml/2 tbsp finely chopped
    fresh parsley
  30ml/2 tbsp finely chopped fresh
    coriander (cilantro)
  30ml/2 tbsp chopped fresh chives
  15ml/1 tbsp chopped fresh dill
  3–4 spring onions (scallions),
    finely chopped
  60ml/4 tbsp butter
  5ml/1 tsp ground cinnamon
  2–3 saffron threads, dissolved in
    15ml/1 tbsp boiling water
  salt

1 Drain the rice, and then boil it in a pan of salted water for 5 minutes, reduce the heat and simmer for 10 minutes.

2 Stir in the chopped herbs and spring onions and mix well with a fork. Simmer for a few minutes more, then drain but do not rinse. Wash and dry the pan.

3 Heat half of the butter in the pan, add 15ml/1 tbsp water, then stir in the rice. Cook over a very low heat for 10 minutes, till almost cooked, then add the remaining butter, the cinnamon and saffron water and cover the pan with a clean towel. Secure a tight-fitting lid, and steam for 30–40 minutes. Serve.

TOP Energy 460Kcal/1924kJ; Protein 8.3g; Carbohydrate 87.2g, of which sugars 19.6g; Fat 8.7g, of which saturates 3.4g; Cholesterol 12mg; Calcium 66mg; Fibre 2.2g; Sodium 79mg.
BOTTOM Energy 435Kcal/1809kJ; Protein 7.3g; Carbohydrate 70.7g, of which sugars 0.8g; Fat 13.1g, of which saturates 7.8g; Cholesterol 32mg; Calcium 61mg; Fibre 1.1g; Sodium 98mg.

MARRAKESH PIZZA

IN MOROCCO, COOKS TEND TO PLACE FLAVOURINGS INSIDE RATHER THAN ON TOP OF THE DOUGH, SO THAT THE FLAVOURS PERMEATE RIGHT THROUGH. THE RESULT IS SURPRISING — AND QUITE DELICIOUS.

MAKES FOUR

INGREDIENTS
5ml/1 tsp sugar
10ml/2 tsp dried yeast
450g/1lb/4 cups strong white
  bread flour
10ml/2 tsp salt
melted butter, for brushing
rocket (arugula) salad and olives, to
  serve
For the filling
1 small onion, very finely chopped
2 tomatoes, skinned, seeded
  and chopped
25ml/1½ tbsp chopped fresh parsley
25ml/1½ tbsp chopped fresh
  coriander (cilantro)
5ml/1 tsp paprika
5ml/1 tsp ground cumin
50g/2oz/⅓ cup shredded vegetable
  suet (chilled, grated shortening)
40g/1½oz Cheddar cheese, grated

1 First prepare the yeast. Place 150ml/ ¼ pint/⅔ cup warm water in a small bowl, stir in the sugar and then sprinkle with the yeast. Stir once or twice, then set aside in a warm place for about 10 minutes until frothy.

2 Meanwhile, make the filling. Mix together the onion, tomatoes, chopped parsley, chopped coriander, paprika, cumin, suet and cheese, then season with salt and set aside.

3 In a large bowl, mix together the flour and 10ml/2 tsp salt. Add the yeast mixture and enough warm water to make a fairly soft dough (about 250ml/ 8fl oz/1 cup). Knead the mixture into a ball and then knead on a floured work surface for 10–12 minutes until the dough is firm and elastic.

4 Divide the dough into four pieces and roll each into a rectangle, measuring 20 x 30cm/8 x 12in. Spread the filling down the centre of each rectangle, then fold into three, to make a rectangle 20 x 10cm/8 x 4in.

5 Roll out the dough again, until it is the same size as before and again fold into three to make a smaller rectangle. (The filling will be squeezed out in places, but don't worry – just push it back inside the dough.)

6 Place the pizzas on a buttered baking sheet, cover with oiled clear film (plastic wrap) and leave in a warm place for about 1 hour until slightly risen.

7 Heat a griddle and brush with butter. Prick the pizzas with a fork five or six times on both sides and then fry for about 8 minutes on each side, until crisp and golden.

8 Serve the pizzas immediately, with a little melted butter if liked, and accompanied by rocket salad and black olives.

Energy 548Kcal/2313kJ; Protein 14.2g; Carbohydrate 92.7g, of which sugars 5.3g; Fat 16g, of which saturates 8g; Cholesterol 11mg; Calcium 259mg; Fibre 4.8g; Sodium 1063mg.

ISRAELI SPICED SEED BREADS

ORANGE FLOWER WATER SCENTS THESE DELICIOUS BREADS, WHICH ARE FLAVOURED WITH SESAME SEEDS AND FENNEL SEEDS. THEY ARE BEST SERVED WARM, WITH BUTTER AND HONEY.

MAKES TWELVE

INGREDIENTS
   5ml/1 tsp sugar
   10ml/2 tsp dried yeast
   75g/3oz/6 tbsp butter, melted
   15ml/1 tbsp orange flower water or
     almond essence (extract) (optional)
   400g/14oz/3½ cups strong white
     bread flour
   75g/3oz/¾ cup icing
     (confectioners') sugar
   5ml/1 tsp salt
   30ml/2 tbsp sesame seeds
   15ml/1 tbsp fennel seeds
   beaten egg, to glaze

1 First start the yeast. Place 120ml/ 4fl oz/½ cup warm water in a jug, stir in the sugar and sprinkle the yeast on top. Stir and then set aside for about 10 minutes until frothy.

2 Place the melted butter, orange flower water or almond essence, and 175ml/ 6fl oz/¾ cup warm water in a separate jug and stir to mix. Stir the flour, icing sugar, salt, sesame seeds and fennel seeds together in the bowl of a food processor fitted with the dough blade.

3 Add the yeast and half of the butter and water mixture to the flour and process so that they slowly combine. Continue processing, adding the remaining butter and water to make a smooth and glossy dough. (You may need to add extra flour/warm water.)

4 Continue processing for 1–2 minutes, then transfer the dough to a floured board and knead by hand for a few minutes until the dough is smooth and elastic.

5 Place in a clean, lightly oiled bowl, cover with clear film (plastic wrap) and leave in a warm place for 1–1½ hours until doubled in size. Knead again for a few minutes and then divide and shape into 12 small balls and flatten slightly with oiled hands. Place on a greased baking sheet, cover with oiled clear film and leave to rise for 1 hour.

6 Preheat the oven to 190°C/375°F/ Gas 5. Brush the breads with beaten egg and then bake for 12–15 minutes, until golden brown. Serve warm or cold.

Energy 201Kcal/847kJ; Protein 3.7g; Carbohydrate 32.8g, of which sugars 7.4g; Fat 7g, of which saturates 3.5g; Cholesterol 13mg; Calcium 68mg; Fibre 1.2g; Sodium 204mg.

PASTRIES AND DESSERTS

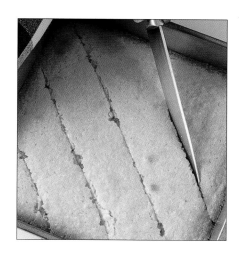  

Some of the world's most sumptuous sweet treats can be found in Middle Eastern pastry shops — filled with fruit or nuts, then fashioned into elaborate shapes, the pastries emerge from the oven to be coated in syrup or honey. Such delights are not intended to be eaten every day. Super-sweet treats like Cheese-filled Jerusalem Kodafa Drenched with Syrup are saved for special occasions, and are eaten in small portions.

BAKLAVA

THE FILLING FOR THIS FAMOUS MIDDLE EASTERN DESSERT CAN BE WALNUTS, ALMONDS OR PISTACHIOS.
THIS VERSION CELEBRATES THE PERSIAN NEW YEAR ON MARCH 21, THE FIRST DAY OF SPRING.

MAKES ABOUT THIRTY-EIGHT TO FORTY

INGREDIENTS
  350g/12oz/3 cups ground
    pistachio nuts
  150g/5oz/1¼ cups icing
    (confectioners') sugar
  15ml/1 tbsp ground cardamom
  150g/5oz/10 tbsp unsalted (sweet)
    butter, melted
  450g/1lb filo pastry
For the syrup
  450g/1lb/2¼ cups sugar
  300ml/½ pint/1¼ cups water
  30ml/2 tbsp rose water

COOK'S TIP
Use ground hazelnuts or almonds instead
of pistachio nuts.

1 First make the syrup. Place the sugar
and water in a pan, bring to the boil,
then simmer for 10 minutes, until
syrupy. Stir in the rose water and then
leave to cool.

2 Mix together the nuts, icing sugar and
cardamom. Preheat the oven to 160°C/
325°F/Gas 3 and brush a large,
rectangular baking tin (pan) with a little
melted butter.

3 Taking one sheet of filo pastry at a
time, and keeping the remainder
covered with a damp cloth, brush the
pastry sheet with melted butter and lay
on the bottom of the tin. Continue until
you have six buttered layers of pastry in
the tin. Spread half of the nut mixture
over the pastry, pressing it down with
a spoon.

4 Take another six sheets of filo pastry,
brush with butter and lay over the nut
mixture. Sprinkle over the remaining
nuts and top with a final layer of six filo
sheets, brushed again with butter. Cut
the pastry diagonally into small lozenge
shapes using a sharp knife. Pour the
remaining melted butter over the top.

5 Bake in the oven for 20 minutes, then
increase the oven temperature to 200°C/
400°F/Gas 6 and bake for a further 15
minutes, until golden and puffed.

6 Remove from the oven and drizzle
about three quarters of the syrup over
the pastry, reserving the remainder for
serving. Arrange the baklava lozenges
on a large glass dish and serve with
extra syrup.

Energy 161kcal/675kJ; Protein 2.3g; Carbohydrate 21.3g, of which sugars 16.3g; Fat 8g, of which saturates 2.6g; Cholesterol 8mg; Calcium 27mg; Fibre 0.7g; Sodium 70mg.

MA'AMOUL

Jews eat these date and nut biscuits at Purim, Christians enjoy them at Easter and Muslims serve them at Iftar, the after-sunset meal that breaks the Ramadan fast.

MAKES THIRTY-FIVE TO FORTY

INGREDIENTS
450g/1lb/4 cups plain
(all-purpose) flour
225g/8oz/1 cup unsalted (sweet)
butter, diced
45ml/3 tbsp rose water
60–75ml/4–5 tbsp milk
icing (confectioners') sugar, for dusting
For the filling
225g/8oz/1⅓ cups dried dates,
stoned (pitted) and chopped
175g/6oz/1 cup walnuts,
finely chopped
115g/4oz/⅔ cup blanched
almonds, chopped
50g/2oz/⅓ cup pistachio nuts,
chopped
120ml/4fl oz/½ cup water
115g/4oz/⅔ cup sugar
10ml/2 tsp ground cinnamon

1 Preheat the oven to 160°C/325°F/ Gas 3. First make the filling. Place the dates, walnuts, almonds, pistachio nuts, water, sugar and cinnamon in a small pan and cook over a low heat, until the dates are soft and the water has been absorbed. Set aside.

2 Place the flour in a bowl and add the butter, working it into the flour with your fingertips. Add the rose water and milk and knead the dough until soft.

3 Take walnut-size pieces of dough. Roll each one into a ball and hollow with your thumb. Pinch the sides.

4 Place a spoonful of date mixture in the hollow then press the dough back over the filling to enclose it, press the edges together to seal.

5 Arrange the pastries on a large baking sheet. Press to flatten them slightly. Make little dents with a fork on the top of the pastries.

6 Bake in the oven for 20 minutes. Do not let them change colour or they will become hard. Cool slightly, and sprinkle with sifted icing sugar.

Energy 186Kcal/775kJ; Protein 3.2g; Carbohydrate 18.4g, of which sugars 8.4g; Fat 11.5g, of which saturates 3.9g; Cholesterol 14mg; Calcium 39mg; Fibre 1.2g; Sodium 49mg.

ALMOND FINGERS

THIS VERY SIMPLE MIDDLE EASTERN SWEETMEAT IS ALSO POPULAR IN TUNISIA. THE FILO IS ROLLED INTO CIGAR SHAPES, WHICH ARE FILLED WITH A GROUND NUT AND ROSE WATER PASTE.

MAKES FORTY TO FIFTY

INGREDIENTS

200g/7oz/1¾ cups ground almonds
50g/2oz/½ cup ground pistachio nuts
50g/2oz/¼ cup sugar
15ml/1 tbsp rose water
2.5ml/½ tsp ground cinnamon
12 sheets of filo pastry
115g/4oz/½ cup butter, melted
icing (confectioners') sugar,
  to decorate

1 Preheat the oven to 160°C/325°F/ Gas 3. Mix together the almonds, pistachio nuts, sugar, rose water and cinnamon for the filling.

2 Cut each sheet of filo pastry into four rectangles. Work with one rectangle at a time, and cover the remaining rectangles with a damp dishtowel to prevent them from drying out.

3 Brush one of the rectangles of filo pastry with a little melted butter and then place a heaped teaspoon of the nut filling in the centre of the pastry.

4 Fold in the sides and roll into a finger or cigar shape. Continue making "cigars" until all the filling and pastry have been used up.

5 Place the fingers on a buttered baking sheet and bake in the oven for 30 minutes, until lightly golden.

6 Transfer to a wire rack to cool and then dust with icing sugar.

COCONUT HALVA

IN EGYPT, THIS SYRUP-SOAKED SWEETMEAT IS CALLED BASBOUSA. TO ACHIEVE THE MOST DELICIOUS STICKINESS, POUR THE COLD SYRUP OVER THE CAKE AS SOON AS IT COMES OUT OF THE OVEN.

SERVES FOUR TO SIX

INGREDIENTS

115g/4oz/½ cup unsalted
  (sweet) butter
175g/6oz/generous ¾ cup sugar
50g/2oz/½ cup plain
  (all-purpose) flour
150g/5oz/scant 1 cup semolina
75g/3oz desiccated (dry
  unsweetened shredded) coconut
175ml/6fl oz/¾ cup milk
5ml/1 tsp baking powder
5ml/1 tsp vanilla extract
whole almonds, to decorate
For the syrup
115g/4oz/⅔ cup caster sugar
150ml/¼ pint/⅔ cup water
15ml/1 tbsp lemon juice

1 First make the syrup. Place the sugar, water and lemon juice in a pan, stir to mix and then bring to the boil and simmer for 6–8 minutes, until it thickens. Allow to cool and then chill.

2 Preheat the oven to 180°C/350°F/ Gas 4. Melt the butter in a pan. Add the sugar, flour, semolina, coconut, milk, baking powder and vanilla extract and mix thoroughly.

3 Pour the cake mixture into a greased shallow baking tin (pan), level the surface and then bake in the oven for 30–35 minutes, until the top is golden.

4 Remove the halva from the oven and cut into diamond-shaped lozenges. Pour the cold syrup evenly over the top and decorate with a whole almond placed in the centre of each lozenge. Serve hot or cold.

TOP Energy 71Kcal/294kJ; Protein 1.5g; Carbohydrate 3.2g, of which sugars 1.6g; Fat 5.9g, of which saturates 1.8g; Cholesterol 6mg; Calcium 17mg; Fibre 0.5g; Sodium 25mg.
BOTTOM Energy 807Kcal/3391kJ; Protein 8.3g; Carbohydrate 118g, of which sugars 79.4g; Fat 36.9g, of which saturates 25.5g; Cholesterol 64mg; Calcium 125mg; Fibre 3.8g; Sodium 208mg.

APRICOT PARCELS WITH HONEY GLAZE

THESE PARCELS CAN BE MADE WITH DRIED APRICOTS THAT HAVE BEEN POACHED IN SYRUP BEFORE BEING STUFFED WITH THE ALMOND MIXTURE, BUT FRESH FRUIT IS THE BETTER OPTION. IT HAS A JUICY TARTNESS THAT CUTS THROUGH THE SWEETNESS OF THE HONEY. ROLL THE FILO PARCELS INTO ANY SHAPE, BUT LEAVE THEM OPEN SO THAT FRUIT AND PASTRY BENEFIT FROM THE GLAZE.

SERVES SIX

INGREDIENTS
    200g/7oz/1¾ cups blanched
      almonds, ground
    115g/4oz/⅔ cup sugar
    30–45ml/2–3 tbsp orange flower
      water or rose water
    12 fresh apricots, slit and
      stoned (pitted)
    3–4 sheets of filo pastry, cut into
      12 circles or squares
    30ml/2 tbsp clear honey

1 Preheat the oven to 180°C/350°F/ Gas 4. Using your hands or a blender or food processor, bind the almonds, sugar and orange flower or rose water to a soft paste.

2 Take small walnut-size lumps of the paste and roll them into balls. Press a ball of paste into each slit apricot and gently squeeze the fruit closed.

3 Place a stuffed apricot on a piece of filo pastry, fold up the sides to secure the fruit and twist the ends to form an open boat. Repeat with the remaining apricots and filo pastry.

4 Place the filo parcels in a shallow ovenproof dish and drizzle the honey over them. Bake for 20–25 minutes, until the pastry is crisp and the fruit has browned on top.

5 Serve hot or cold with cream, crème fraîche, or a spoonful of yogurt.

Energy 347Kcal/1455kJ; Protein 9g; Carbohydrate 37.8g, of which sugars 27.4g; Fat 18.9g, of which saturates 1.5g; Cholesterol 0mg; Calcium 120mg; Fibre 4.2g; Sodium 8mg.

M'HANNCHA

The snake, or m'hanncha to use the Arabic name, is the most famous sweet dish in Morocco. The coiled pastry looks impressive and tastes superb. Crisp, buttery filo is filled with almond paste that has been spiced with cinnamon and scented with orange flower water. Serve m'hanncha as a dessert or as an afternoon treat with mint tea.

SERVES EIGHT TO TEN

INGREDIENTS
115g/4oz/⅔ cup blanched almonds
115g/4oz/½ cup butter, softened,
  plus 20g/¾oz for cooking nuts
300g/11oz/2⅔ cups ground almonds
50g/2oz/½ cup icing
  (confectioners') sugar
115g/4oz/⅔ cup caster
  (superfine) sugar
5–10ml/1–2 tsp ground cinnamon
15ml/1 tbsp orange flower water
3–4 sheets of filo pastry
melted butter, for brushing
1 egg yolk
icing (confectioner's) sugar and
  ground cinnamon for the topping

1 Fry the blanched almonds in a little butter until golden brown, then pound them using a pestle and mortar until they resemble coarse breadcrumbs.

2 Place the nuts in a bowl and add the ground almonds, icing sugar, caster sugar, softened butter, cinnamon and orange flower water. Use your hands to form the mixture into a smooth paste. Cover and chill for 30 minutes.

3 Preheat the oven to 180°C/350°F/ Gas 4. Grease a large, round baking tin (pan) or a wide baking sheet.

4 Open out the sheets of filo pastry, keeping them in a pile so they do not dry out, and brush the top one with a little melted butter.

5 Lift one of the filo rolls in both hands and push it together from both ends, like an accordion, to relax the pastry before coiling it in the centre of the tin or baking sheet. Do the same with the other rolls, placing them end to end to form a tight coil like a snake.

6 Take lumps of the almond paste and roll them into fingers. Place them end to end along the long edge of the top sheet of filo, then roll the filo up into a roll the thickness of your thumb, tucking in the ends to stop the filling oozing out.

7 Repeat this with the other sheets of filo, until all the filling is used up.

8 Mix the egg yolk with a little water and brush this over the pastry, then bake in the oven for 30–35 minutes, until crisp and lightly browned.

9 Top the freshly cooked pastry with a liberal sprinkling of icing sugar, and add lines of cinnamon like the spokes of a wheel. Serve at room temperature.

Energy 281Kcal/1168kJ; Protein 4.1g; Carbohydrate 21g, of which sugars 15.8g; Fat 20.6g, of which saturates 8.3g; Cholesterol 56mg; Calcium 56mg; Fibre 1.3g; Sodium 91mg.

FRESH FIG, APPLE <u>AND</u> DATE SALAD

FIGS AND DATES COMBINE ESPECIALLY WELL WITH CRISP DESSERT APPLES. USE FRESH FIGS IF YOU CAN FIND THEM. A HINT OF ALMOND SERVES TO UNITE THE FLAVOURS.

SERVES FOUR

INGREDIENTS

6 large apples
juice of ½ lemon
175g/6oz fresh dates
25g/1oz white marzipan
5ml/1 tsp orange flower water
60ml/4 tbsp natural (plain)
 yogurt
4 green or purple figs
4 toasted almonds, to decorate

1 Core the apples. Slice thinly, then cut them into fine matchsticks. Moisten with lemon juice to keep them white.

2 Remove the stones from the dates and cut the flesh into fine strips, then combine them with the apple slices.

3 Soften the white marzipan with orange flower water and combine it with the yogurt. Mix well.

4 Pile the apples and dates in the centre of four plates. Remove the stem from each of the figs and divide the fruit into quarters, without cutting right through the base.

5 Squeeze the base with the thumb and forefinger of each hand to open up the fruit.

6 Place a fig in the centre of the salad, spoon in the yogurt filling and decorate with a toasted almond.

Energy 185kcal/790kJ; Protein 2.9g; Carbohydrate 43g, of which sugars 43g; Fat 1.5g, of which saturates 0.2g; Cholesterol 0mg; Calcium 99mg; Fibre 4.8g; Sodium 32mg.

ORANGE AND DATE SALAD

FRESH DATES ARE BEST FOR THIS FRAGRANT SALAD. IT IS POPULAR THROUGHOUT THE ARAB WORLD, AND CAN BE SERVED AS A DESSERT OR AS AN ACCOMPANIMENT TO ROASTED MEATS.

SERVES FOUR TO SIX

INGREDIENTS
    6 oranges
    15–30ml/1–2 tbsp orange flower
      water or rose water (optional)
    lemon juice (optional)
    115g/4oz/⅔ cup stoned (pitted)
      dates (see Cook's Tip)
    50g/2oz/⅓ cup pistachio nuts
    icing (confectioners') sugar,
      to taste
    a few whole blanched almonds

COOK'S TIP
Use fresh dates, if you can find them, although dried dates are delicious in this salad, too.

1 Peel the oranges with a sharp knife, removing all the pith, and cut into segments, catching the juices in a bowl. Place the orange segments in a serving dish.

2 Stir in the juice from the bowl together with a little orange flower or rose water, if using, and sharpen with lemon juice, if liked.

3 Chop the dates and pistachio nuts and sprinkle over the salad with a little sifted icing sugar. Chill in the refrigerator for 1 hour.

4 Just before serving, sprinkle over the toasted almonds and a little extra icing sugar and serve.

Energy 156Kcal/655kJ; Protein 4.4g; Carbohydrate 19.9g, of which sugars 19.6g; Fat 7.1g, of which saturates 0.9g; Cholesterol 0mg; Calcium 101mg; Fibre 4g; Sodium 76mg.

ORANGES IN SYRUP

BOTH BITTER AND SWEET ORANGES ARE EXTENSIVELY CULTIVATED IN THE MIDDLE EAST. THIS METHOD OF SERVING THEM, IN SYRUP SCENTED WITH ORANGE BLOSSOM OR ROSE, IS VERY POPULAR.

SERVES FOUR

INGREDIENTS
4 oranges
600ml/1 pint/2½ cups water
350g/12oz/1¾ cups sugar
30ml/2 tbsp lemon juice
30ml/2 tbsp orange flower water
  or rose water
50g/2oz/½ cup chopped
  pistachio nuts, to decorate

VARIATION
Substitute almonds for the pistachio nuts.

1 Peel the oranges with a potato peeler down to the pith.

2 Cut the orange peel into fine strips and then boil in water, changing the water several times to remove the bitterness. Drain and set aside until required.

3 Place the water, sugar and lemon juice in a pan. Bring to the boil and add the orange peel. Simmer until the syrup thickens. Stir in the orange flower or rose water, and leave to cool.

4 Completely cut the pith away from the oranges and cut into thick slices. Place in a shallow serving dish and pour over the syrup.

5 Chill for about 1–2 hours. Decorate with pistachio nuts and serve.

Energy 120Kcal/500kJ; Protein 3.6g; Carbohydrate 11.2g, of which sugars 10.9g; Fat 7.1g, of which saturates 0.9g; Cholesterol 0mg; Calcium 70mg; Fibre 2.8g; Sodium 72mg.

PAPAYA AND MANGO WITH MANGO CREAM

MAKE THE MOST OF MANGOES WHEN THEY ARE IN SEASON BY MIXING THEM WITH PAPAYAS AND TOSSING THEM IN AN APRICOT SAUCE. A CHILLED MANGO CREAM IS THE PERFECT TOPPING.

SERVES FOUR

INGREDIENTS

2 large ripe mangoes
300ml/½ pint/1¼ cups extra thick double (heavy) cream
8 ready-to-eat dried apricots, halved
150ml/¼ pint/⅔ cup orange juice or water
1 ripe papaya

1 Take one thick slice from one of the mangoes and, while still on the skin, slash the flesh with a sharp knife in a criss-cross pattern to make cubes.

2 Turn the piece of mango inside-out and cut away the cubed flesh from the skin. Place the flesh in a bowl, mash with a fork to a pulp, then add the cream and mix together. Spoon into a freezer-proof container, cover and freeze for about 1–1½ hours, until half frozen.

3 Put the apricots and orange juice or water in a small pan. Bring to the boil, then simmer gently until the apricots are soft, adding a little juice or water, if necessary, to keep moist. Remove the pan from the heat and set aside to cool.

4 Peel, stone (pit) and chop or dice the remaining mango as before and place in a bowl. Cut the papaya in half, remove and discard the seeds and peel. Dice the flesh and add to the mango.

5 Pour the apricot sauce over the fruit and gently toss together so the fruit is well coated.

6 Stir the semi-frozen mango cream a few times until it is spoonable but not soft. Serve the fruit topped with the mango cream.

COOK'S TIP

Mangoes vary tremendously in size. If you can only find small ones, buy three instead of two to use in this dessert.

Energy 462Kcal/1914kJ; Protein 2.6g; Carbohydrate 23g, of which sugars 22.8g; Fat 40.6g, of which saturates 25.1g; Cholesterol 103mg; Calcium 67mg; Fibre 3.6g; Sodium 26mg.

CHEESE-FILLED JERUSALEM KODAFA DRENCHED <u>WITH</u> SYRUP

IN JERUSALEM, AS ELSEWHERE IN THE MIDDLE EAST, THIS SUPER-SWEET PASTRY IS A POPULAR STREET FOOD AND YOU WILL OFTEN SEE KODAFA VENDORS WEAVING THROUGH THE TRAFFIC WITH LARGE TRAYS OF THE SWEETMEAT BALANCED ON THEIR HEADS. KODAFA IS USUALLY MADE WITH A SHREDDED PASTRY CALLED KADAIF. THIS VERSION USES COUSCOUS, WHICH GIVES AN EQUALLY TASTY RESULT.

SERVES SIX

INGREDIENTS

- 200–250g/7–9oz/1–1½ cup couscous
- 525ml/17fl oz/2¼ cups boiling water
- 130–200g/4½–7oz/½–1 cup butter, cut into small pieces
- 1 egg, lightly beaten
- pinch of salt
- 400g/14oz/1¾ cups ricotta cheese
- 175–200g/6–7oz cheese, such as mozzarella, Taleggio or Monterey Jack, grated or finely chopped
- 350ml/12fl oz/1½ cups clear honey
- 2–3 pinches of saffron threads or ground cinnamon
- 120ml/4fl oz/½ cup water
- 5ml/1 tsp orange flower water or lemon juice
- 90ml/6 tbsp roughly chopped pistachio nuts

1 Put the couscous in a large bowl and pour over the boiling water. Stir together with a fork, then leave to soak for about 30 minutes, until the water has been completely absorbed.

2 When the couscous is cool enough to handle, break up all the lumps with your fingers.

3 Stir the butter into the couscous, then stir in the beaten egg and salt.

4 Preheat the oven to 200°C/400°F/ Gas 6. Spread half the couscous into a 25–30cm/10–12in round cake tin (pan).

5 In a bowl, combine the cheeses and 30ml/2 tbsp of the honey. Spread the cheese mixture on top of the couscous, then top with the remaining couscous. Press down gently and then bake in the oven for 10–15 minutes.

6 Meanwhile, put the remaining honey, the saffron threads or cinnamon, and the water in a pan. Bring to the boil, then boil for 5–7 minutes, until the liquid forms a syrup. Remove from the heat and stir in the orange flower water or lemon juice.

7 Preheat the grill (broiler) to its hottest setting. When the kodafa is cooked, place it under the grill and cook until it is lightly browned on top and a golden crust is formed.

8 Sprinkle the pistachio nuts on top of the kodafa. Serve warm, cut into wedges, with the syrup.

VARIATIONS

Other versions of this pastry are made with biscuit (cookie) crumbs and broken pistachio nuts. If you like, warm this kodafa through in the microwave before serving it with strong coffee or mint tea.

Energy 702Kcal/2927kJ; Protein 17.6g; Carbohydrate 65.1g, of which sugars 47.6g; Fat 43g, of which saturates 22.7g; Cholesterol 123mg; Calcium 140mg; Fibre 0.9g; Sodium 344mg.

SAFFRON AND CARDAMOM CRÈME CARAMEL WITH BUTTER COOKIES

MANY OF THE CHILLED CREAMY CUSTARDS, MILK PUDDINGS AND RICE PUDDINGS THAT ARE SERVED IN THE MIDDLE EAST ARE FAMILIAR TO VISITORS FROM EUROPE, BUT THERE ARE SUBTLE VARIATIONS. FLAVOURING OFTEN COMES FROM SPICES LIKE SAFFRON OR CARDAMOM, OR FROM FLORAL ESSENCES LIKE ROSE WATER OR ORANGE FLOWER WATER.

SERVES FOUR TO SIX

INGREDIENTS
  600ml/1 pint/2½ cups milk
  115g/4oz/⅔ cup sugar, plus
    60ml/4 tbsp for caramel
  pinch of saffron threads
  2.5ml/½ tsp cardamom seeds
  15–30ml/1–2 tbsp rose water
  4 eggs, lightly beaten
  60ml/4 tbsp boiling water
For the cookies
  200g/7oz/scant 1 cup butter
  130g/4½oz/generous 1 cup icing
    (confectioners') sugar, sifted
  5–10ml/1–2 tsp orange flower water
  250g/9oz/2¼ cups plain (all-purpose)
    flour, sifted
  handful of whole blanched almonds

1 Preheat the oven to 180°C/350°F/ Gas 4. Heat the milk, sugar, saffron and cardamom in a pan until the milk is just about to boil. Remove the pan from the heat and set aside to cool. Add the rose water, then gradually pour the mixture on to the eggs in a bowl, beating all the time. Set aside.

2 To make the caramel, heat the 60ml/ 4 tbsp sugar in a small, heavy pan, until melted and dark brown. Stir in the water, holding the pan at arm's length as the caramel will spit. Let it bubble before pouring it into individual ovenproof dishes. Swirl the dishes to coat the base and sides evenly. Leave to cool.

3 Pour the custard into the dishes and then stand them in a roasting pan. Pour in enough cold water to come two-thirds of the way up the outsides of the dishes.

4 Bake in the oven for about 1 hour, or until the custard has set. Cool, then chill in the refrigerator for several hours or overnight.

5 To make the cookies, melt the butter in a pan and then leave to cool until lukewarm. Stir in the icing sugar and orange flower water, then gradually beat in the flour to form a smooth, stiff dough. Wrap in clear film (plastic wrap) and chill for 15 minutes.

6 Preheat the oven to 180°C/350°F/ Gas 4. Grease a baking sheet. Break off walnut-size pieces of dough and roll them into balls. Place on the baking sheet and flatten slightly. Press a whole blanched almond into the centre of each. Bake for 20 minutes, or until golden. Allow to cool slightly on the baking sheet; when firm, transfer to a wire rack.

7 To serve, run a knife around the edges of the crème caramel dishes and invert on to plates. Serve immediately with the butter cookies.

Energy 969Kcal/4064kJ; Protein 17.8g; Carbohydrate 119.9g, of which sugars 72.3g; Fat 50g, of which saturates 29.3g; Cholesterol 306mg; Calcium 338mg; Fibre 2g; Sodium 443mg.

YOGURT CAKE <u>WITH</u> PISTACHIO NUTS, CRÈME FRAÎCHE <u>AND</u> PASSION FRUIT

ONE OF THE MIDDLE EAST'S FAVOURITE INGREDIENTS, YOGURT, IS USED TO MAKE A BEAUTIFULLY MOIST CAKE WITH A CRUNCHY PISTACHIO TOPPING. IT IS DELICIOUS HOT OR COLD, WITH A DOLLOP OF CRÈME FRAÎCHE. FRESH PASSION FRUIT PULP ADDS A TANGY NOTE, BUT THIS WOULD TASTE JUST AS GOOD WITH AN APRICOT COMPOTE OR A SPOONFUL OF TURKISH-STYLE SOUR CHERRY PRESERVE.

SERVES FOUR TO SIX

INGREDIENTS

   3 eggs, separated
   75g/3oz/scant ½ cup caster
    (superfine) sugar
   seeds from 2 vanilla pods (beans)
   300ml/½ pint/1¼ cups Greek
    (US strained plain) yogurt
   grated rind and juice of 1 lemon
   scant 15ml/1 tbsp plain
    (all-purpose) flour
   handful of pistachio nuts,
    roughly chopped
   60–90ml/4–6 tbsp crème fraîche and
    4–6 fresh passion fruit or
    50g/2oz/½ cup summer berries,
    to serve

1 Preheat the oven to 180°C/350°F/ Gas 4. Line a 25cm/10in square, ovenproof dish with greaseproof (waxed) paper and grease well.

2 Beat the egg yolks with two-thirds of the sugar in a bowl, until pale and fluffy. Beat in the vanilla seeds and then stir in the yogurt, lemon rind and juice, and the flour. In a separate bowl, whisk the egg whites until stiff, then gradually whisk in the rest of the sugar to form soft peaks. Fold the whisked whites into the yogurt mixture. Turn the mixture into the prepared dish.

3 Place the dish in a roasting pan and pour in enough cold water to come about halfway up the outside of the dish. Bake in the oven for about 20 minutes, until the mixture is risen and just set. Sprinkle the pistachio nuts over the cake and then bake for a further 20 minutes, until browned on top.

4 Serve the cake warm or cooled and chilled, with crème fraîche and a spoonful of passion fruit drizzled over the top. Alternatively, sprinkle with a few summer berries such as redcurrants, blackcurrants and blueberries.

Energy 474Kcal/1986kJ; Protein 13.4g; Carbohydrate 49.4g, of which sugars 46g; Fat 26.3g, of which saturates 10g; Cholesterol 170mg; Calcium 195mg; Fibre 2.2g; Sodium 283mg.

GRILLED FRUIT WITH WATERMELON

FOR THIS STUNNING DESSERT, SLICED FRESH PINEAPPLE AND MANGO ARE CARAMELIZED ALONGSIDE HALVED BANANAS BEFORE BEING SERVED WITH A CHOICE OF TWO GRANITAS, ONE MADE FROM PURÉED WATERMELON AND THE OTHER A SPICY ORANGE, CLOVE AND GINGER CONCOCTION.

SERVES SIX TO EIGHT

INGREDIENTS
  1 pineapple
  1 mango
  2 bananas
  45–60ml/3–4 tbsp icing
    (confectioners') sugar
For the watermelon granita
  1kg/2¼lb watermelon, seeds removed
  250g/9oz/1¼ cups caster
    (superfine) sugar
  150ml/¼ pint/⅔ cup water
  juice of ½ lemon
  15ml/1 tbsp orange flower water
  2.5ml/½ tsp ground cinnamon

For the spiced orange granita
  900ml/1½ pints/3¾ cups water
  350g/12oz/1¾ cups caster
    (superfine) sugar
  5–6 whole cloves
  5ml/1 tsp ground ginger
  2.5ml/½ tsp ground cinnamon
  600ml/1 pint/2½ cups fresh
    orange juice
  15ml/1 tbsp orange flower water

1 To make the watermelon granita, purée the watermelon flesh in a blender. Put the sugar and water in a pan and stir until dissolved. Bring to the boil, simmer for 5 minutes, then cool.

2 Stir in the lemon juice, orange flower water and cinnamon, then beat in the watermelon purée. Pour the mixture into a bowl and place it in the freezer. Stir every 15 minutes for 2 hours and then at intervals for 1 hour, so that the mixture freezes but is slushy.

3 To make the spiced orange granita, heat the water and sugar together in a pan with the cloves, stirring until the sugar has dissolved, then bring to the boil and boil for about 5 minutes. Remove from the heat, leave to cool and then stir in the ginger, cinnamon, orange juice and orange flower water.

4 Remove and discard the cloves, then pour the mixture into a bowl, cover and place in the freezer. Freeze in the same way as the watermelon granita.

5 To serve, peel, core and slice the pineapple. Peel the mango, cut the flesh off the stone (pit) in thick slices. Peel and halve the bananas. Preheat the grill (broiler) on the hottest setting. Arrange the fruit on a baking sheet. Sprinkle with icing sugar and grill (broil) for 3–4 minutes, until slightly softened and lightly browned. Arrange the fruit on a serving platter and scoop the granitas into dishes. Serve immediately.

Energy 606Kcal/2585kJ; Protein 2.9g; Carbohydrate 156.2g, of which sugars 155.5g; Fat 1g, of which saturates 0.2g; Cholesterol 0mg; Calcium 107mg; Fibre 2.8g; Sodium 23mg.

TURKISH DELIGHT SORBET

LOVE TURKISH DELIGHT, BUT DON'T WANT STICKY FINGERS? SERVE THIS SUPERB SORBET INSTEAD. IT HAS ALL THE FLAVOUR AND AROMA OF THE SWEETMEAT FROM WHICH IT IS MADE, BUT IS EASIER TO EAT. SERVE IT IN SMALL PORTIONS WITH A POT OF STRONG COFFEE.

SERVES FOUR

INGREDIENTS
    250g/9oz rose water-flavoured
      Turkish delight
    30ml/2 tbsp sugar
    750ml/1¼ pints/3 cups water
    30ml/2 tbsp lemon juice
    50g/2oz white chocolate, broken
      into squares
    roughly chopped almonds,
      to decorate

1 Cut the Turkish delight into small pieces with a pair of scissors. Put half the pieces in a heavy pan with the sugar. Pour in half the water. Heat gently until the Turkish delight has dissolved, stirring.

2 Cool, then stir in the lemon juice with the remaining water and Turkish delight. Chill in the refrigerator for several hours.

3 By hand: Pour the mixture into a shallow freezerproof container and freeze for 3–4 hours, beating twice as it thickens. Return to the freezer until ready to serve.
Using an ice cream maker: Churn the mixture until it holds its shape.

4 While the sorbet is freezing, dampen eight very small plastic cups or glasses, then line them with clear film (plastic wrap).

5 Spoon the sorbet into the cups and tap them lightly on the surface to compact the mixture. Cover with the overlapping clear film and freeze for at least 3 hours or overnight.

6 Make a paper piping bag. Put the chocolate in a heatproof bowl and melt it over a pan of gently simmering water. Remove the sorbets from the freezer, let them stand for 5 minutes, then pull them out of the cups.

7 Transfer to serving plates and peel off the clear film. Spoon the melted chocolate into the piping bag, snip off the tip and scribble a design on the sorbet and the plate. Sprinkle the almonds over the top and serve.

Energy 280Kcal/1188kJ; Protein 1.4g; Carbohydrate 63.8g, of which sugars 58g; Fat 3.9g, of which saturates 2.3g; Cholesterol 0mg; Calcium 44mg; Fibre 0g; Sodium 34mg.

SWEET PUDDING

WITH ITS DELICATE FLAVOUR AND SILKY SMOOTH TEXTURE, THIS MILK PUDDING WOULD MAKE THE PERFECT FINALE FOR A MIDDLE EASTERN MEAL. STREW THE PLATE WITH ROSE PETALS, IF YOU LIKE.

SERVES FOUR

INGREDIENTS

50g/2oz/⅓ cup ground rice
45ml/3 tbsp cornflour (cornstarch)
1.2 litres/2 pints/5 cups milk
75g/3oz/scant ½ cup sugar
30ml/2 tbsp rose water
50g/2oz/½ cup ground almonds
25g/1oz/¼ cup ground pistachio nuts
ground cinnamon, to decorate
golden (light corn) syrup or clear
   honey, warmed, to serve

1 Blend the ground rice and cornflour to a paste with a little cold milk in a small bowl. Set aside.

2 Bring the remaining milk to the boil in a pan, then add the sugar and simmer gently. Gradually add the ground rice paste to the milk, stirring constantly with a wooden spoon to mix.

3 Simmer the mixture over a very gentle heat for 10–15 minutes, until the mixture has thickened, stirring frequently and being very careful not to burn the bottom of the pan, which would damage the very delicate flavour of the rice.

4 Stir in the rose water and half of the ground almonds and simmer for a further 5 minutes.

5 Cool for a few minutes and then pour the rice mixture into a serving bowl or individual dishes.

6 Sprinkle with the remaining ground almonds and ground pistachio nuts and then decorate with a dusting of ground cinnamon. Serve with warmed syrup or honey.

Energy 409Kcal/1724kJ; Protein 14.7g; Carbohydrate 55.6g, of which sugars 34.8g; Fat 15.6g, of which saturates 4.6g; Cholesterol 18mg; Calcium 395mg; Fibre 1.2g; Sodium 235mg.

MINT TEA

In Morocco, where it is the national drink, mint tea is known as atay bi nahna. The mint leaves are left to infuse in the sweet brew so that the flavour is pronounced.

SERVES TWO

INGREDIENTS
    10ml/2 tsp Chinese gunpowder
      green tea
    small bunch of fresh mint leaves
    sugar, to taste

1 Put the tea in a small tea pot and fill with boiling water. Add the mint leaves and leave it to infuse (steep) for 2–3 minutes.

2 Stir in sugar to taste and pour into tea glasses or cups to serve.

COOK'S TIPS
At feasts and on special occasions, the making of mint tea can be an elaborate ceremony: the best green tea is chosen and only fresh spearmint (*Mentha spicata*), of which a well-known cultivar called Moroccan is used. A fine silver-plated, bulbous-shaped teapot is selected for brewing and the heavily sweetened tea is poured rhythmically into fine glasses. For an additional flounce of ceremony, a fresh, fragrant orange blossom or jasmine flower may be floated in each glass. In winter, wormwood is sometimes added for extra warmth, and infusions flavoured with aniseed or verbena are quite common.

Energy 20Kcal/86kJ; Protein 0.2g; Carbohydrate 5.2g, of which sugars 5.2g; Fat 0g, of which saturates 0g; Cholesterol 0mg; Calcium 3mg; Fibre 0g; Sodium 1mg.

INDEX